THE SHATTERED LANTERN

The Shattered Lantern

Rediscovering a Felt Presence of God

Ronald Rolheiser, O.M.I.

A Crossroad Book
The Crossroad Publishing Company
New York

The Crossroad Publishing Company
481 Eighth Avenue, New York, NY 10001

This edition: copyight © 2004 Ronald Rolheiser
Reflection Guide copyright © 2004 by The Crossroad Publishing
Company
First published in Great Britain in 1994 by Hodder & Stoughton Ltd

Permission to quote the poems on pp. 150 and 175 is gratefully
acknowledged.

Library of Congress Cataloging-in-Publication Data

Rolheiser, Ronald.
   The shattered lantern : rediscovering a felt presence of God /
Ronald Rolheiser.
     p. cm.
Includes bibliographical references.
ISBN 0-8245-2275-3 (alk. paper)
1. Contemplation. I. Title.
BV5091.C7R65 2001
248.8'6—dc22

                                        2004002420

      1   2   3   4   5   6   7   8   9   10   08   07   06   05   04

I dedicate this book to my mother and father,
Mathilda and George,
who taught me never to ridicule anyone
who is searching for God
with a lighted lantern.

Contents

Preface

Imagine lying in bed one night and finding yourself flooded with warm feelings of faith. In that graced moment you truly feel the reality of God. There are no doubts in your mind this night; you know that God exists as surely as you know that you exist. Your faith feels sure.

Now imagine a very different scenario: You wake up one night overwhelmed by feelings of chaos, emptiness, doubt. Try as you might, you can no longer envision the existence of God or convince yourself that you believe. You try to imagine God's existence, feel God's reality, but you draw a blank and your heart fills with the sense that all you've believed in is nothing but wishful thinking. Your heart tells you the heavens are empty. You stare holes into the darkness and all that stares back is darkness, nothingness, emptiness.

Does this mean that on the one night your faith is strong and on the other that it is weak? Is faith a matter of being able to imagine or feel that God exists? Not necessarily. Perhaps all it means is that on the one night you had a strong imagination and on the other a weak one. Faith is not the same thing as being able to imagine God's existence or even of being able to feel God on an emotional level. The mind is mostly unequal to the task of imagining God's existence and the heart is often just as inept at giving us any feeling of it. But God doesn't cease to exist for that reason, nor is faith dead just because the imagination and the heart have run dry. God exists, independent of our perceptions. Faith is something deeper.

We live in a culture that, for the most part, no longer imagines God's existence and concludes that this means both that the culture has lost its faith and that God doesn't exist. This notion is present everywhere. Who among us doesn't have a spouse, a brother, a sister, a child, a close friend, a colleague, a neighbor, or an acquaintance who is not, consciously or unconsciously, convinced that God doesn't exist because he or she can no longer conjure Him up?

I suspect that this is true to a certain extent for each of us. We live lives of quiet agnosticism. Our faith often feels like doubt. Our everyday consciousness contains little or no awareness of God. We tend to be atheistic in our imaginations and in our feelings, even as we profess faith, say the creed, go to church, and perhaps even do ministry. We have icons in our churches but not in our hearts. This is not because we are hedonistic, pagan, bad, or materialistic, but because we live and move and breathe in a culture that no longer gives us the tools to create these icons. Our present cultural currency, certainly in the Western world, is not equipped to help us imagine or feel God's existence. The air we breathe is agnostic, even atheistic. Why is this so?

A good place to begin an examination is with Friedrich Nietzsche's infamous declaration more than a hundred years ago that "God is dead!" Nietzsche put these words into the mouth of a madman who shouts them angrily in a crowded market square as he smashes a lit lantern at high noon. That brief phrase, "God is dead," is usually all that is quoted from that infamous speech, but Nietzsche's madman continues with a crucial indictment and a haunting question: "God is dead! And we are his murderers! With what kind of sponge did we wipe away an entire horizon?"

How did this happen? How did we move from a culture and consciousness dominated by a sense of God's existence to a situation in which we lack the very mental capability to think of, imagine, and feel God's existence? How *did* we murder God? How *did* we wipe away an entire horizon?

This book—which takes its title from what Nietzsche's madman does when he declares that God is dead, shatters a lantern—is for those among us who too frequently catch ourselves having to pray like Peter in the Gospels: "Lord, I believe, but help my unbelief!" It wrestles with both the demons and the angels that lie in the underbrush of that struggle, the problem of unbelief among believers.

Why is it a struggle to imagine and feel God's existence? What is culpable and what is normal in that struggle? Can we murder God by the way we live? What is the route back? Can we resurrect it? What should we do as believers in a culture of agnosticism?

This book does not try to answer all those questions. No book can. Only a life of honesty that wrestles daily with these issues and walks humbly and haltingly within the mystery of it all will finally yield for us the treasure that lies in the answers. This book tries to give some perspectives on how to do that, so that our faith becomes not an act of will but a habit of the heart.

Ron Rolheiser, O.M.I.
Rome, Italy
October 1, 2000

Acknowledgments

Many people have supported me in the writing of this book.

I thank first of all my religious community, the Oblates of Mary Immaculate, who, despite my shortcomings, never waver in how much they trust me and how much they entrust to me. The same is true of my family, that large clan of brothers and sisters and nephews and nieces whose patience with me knows no bounds. A special thanks to Tony Dummer, O.M.I., and the Oblates in Oakland, California, who provided me with the kind of hospitality that makes for a good space within which to write a book—good fellowship, a well-laden table, a daily Eucharist, and a beautiful old room with a hardwood floor and a bay window.

A huge thanks, too, to the warm and wonderful folks at Crossroad Publishing, especially to Gwendolin Herder and Paul McMahon, for adopting this exile.

Part I

=============== ⬥ ===============

Narcissism, Pragmatism,
Unbridled Restlessness, and the Loss
of the Ancient Instinct for Astonishment

===================================

"The greatest of all illusions
is the illusion of familiarity."
—G. K. Chesterton

one

The Problem of Unbelief among Believers

The Agnosticism of Our Ordinary Consciousness

One of the most famous novels of all time begins with the words: "All happy families resemble each other, each unhappy family is unhappy in its own way."[1]

What is true of families is also true of generations, each unique in its unhappiness. Ours is no exception, particularly in its religious struggles. Where past generations of believers unhappily fought over questions of church, of interpretation of scripture, and of the uniqueness and place of Christ, our own religious struggle focuses on the most central question, the existence of God.

We live in an age of unbelief. What sets us apart from past generations is that, today, this is as true within religious circles as outside them. The problem of faith is especially one of unbelief among believers.

Belief in God, for many of us, is little more than a hangover. We feel the effects of the religious activity of the past, but our own consciousness borders on agnosticism. Rarely is there a vital sense of God within the bread and butter of life. We still make a space for God in our churches, but He is given a very restricted place everywhere else.

A hundred years ago, when Friedrich Nietzsche made his declaration that God is dead, he was not suggesting that God in the heavens had died. He was saying that God no longer mattered in everyday life. God is dead, he said, but his "shadow is a long one, and we must first conquer this shadow."[2]

Contemporary analyst Philip Rieff says much the same thing. In his view, our generation has an ambivalent relationship toward God: God has disappeared but we still have his calling card. He is absent but, because of our religious past, we still have a sense of him. Future generations, he asserts, will not even have that.[3]

These images, of faith as a hangover, of religion as struggling with God's shadow, of an absent God whose calling card we still possess, describe in a general way our everyday struggle with faith and agnosticism. We still have some experience of God, though rarely is it a vital one in which we actually drink, first-hand, from living waters. Insofar as God does enter our everyday experience, most often He is not experienced as a living person to whom we actually talk, from whom we seek ultimate consolation and comfort, and to whom we relate person to person, friend to friend, lover to lover, child to parent.

Rather God is experienced and related to as a religion, a church, a moral philosophy, a guide for private virtue, an imperative for justice, or a nostalgia for propriety. For most of us, belief in God resembles the following: God is religion and religion represents a way of life–churchgoing, guidance from the Bible, sex within monogamous marriage; no lying, cheating or swearing, democratic principles, proper aesthetics, and being nice to each other.

God, then, is more of a moral and intellectual principle than a person, and our commitment to this principle runs the gamut from fiery passion, by which people are willing to die for a cause, to a vague nostalgia, in which God and religion are given the same kind of status as the royal family in England—namely, the symbolic anchor of a certain way of life, but hardly important to its day-to-day functioning. It is not that this is bad, it is just that there is little evidence in it that anyone is actually all that interested in God. We are interested in virtue, justice, a proper way of life, and perhaps even in building communities for worship, support, and justice. But, in the end, moral philosophies, human instinct, and a not-so-disguised self-interest are more important in motivating these activities than are love and gratitude stemming from a personal relationship with a living God. God is not only often absent in our marketplaces, he is frequently absent from our religious activities and religious fervor as well.

There is more than a little unbelief among us believers. God is a neurosis, a religion, a cause . . . and only rarely a living, informing, comforting, challenging person whose reality dwarfs that of our everyday world.

Nietzsche presents this scenario in his book *The Gay Science*. A madman lights a lantern and, in bright daylight, rushes into a crowded marketplace shouting: "I seek God! I seek God!"[4] But the people in the marketplace ridicule him. "Has he got lost?" asks one. "Did he lose his way like a child?" asks another. "Is he hiding? Or is he afraid of us?" They yell and laugh at him. Then the madman turns on them and shouts, "God is dead, I tell you, we have killed him, you and I. All of us are his murderers. But how did we do this? How could we drink up the sea? Who gave us the sponge to wipe away the entire horizon? What was the holiest and mightiest of all that the world has yet owned has bled to death under our knives." Then he goes silent, smashes his lantern on the ground, and announces: "I have come too early. This deed is still too distant for people to see, and yet they have done this to themselves. They have killed God!"

How can someone kill God? What Nietzsche suggests in this parable is that unbelief, a kind of atheism, is not something that exists primarily outside the circle of people who take themselves as believers. It is a phenomenon within the circle of believers. The problem of atheism and unbelief is not that the existence of God is denied, but that God is absent from the ordinary consciousness and lives of believers, not alive enough alive or important enough. It is in this way that "we have killed him."

Why is this? Why is God not more alive within our ordinary lives and consciousness? Two explanations exist. Both have their conscientious presenters.

John of the Cross once wrote that a silence of God can occur within experience because God can be "obscure" or because we can be "blind" . . . an object can be vague because it is too distant or because we have bad eyesight.[5] Hence, God can withdraw his presence in order to purify our faith (John's "obscurity"), or we can have a weak experience of God because there is something wrong with us (John's "blindness"). The former he calls "a dark night of the soul," the latter, a fault in contemplation.

Recent theological debate has polarized around this very distinction. Conservatives and liberals both agree that our experience of God today is far from what it could be. After this they differ. Conservatives by and large attribute the problem to what John of the Cross termed "blindness": there is something wrong with the way we are living and this makes the experience of God difficult to attain. Liberals, on the other hand, tend to understand the issue as one of "obscurity." Our experience of God is weak because we are being purified and led through a dark night of the soul to a more mature experience of God. Who is right?

Both of these states operate simultaneously. Always, in every age, we will struggle with faith both because God positively tests us by withdrawing His consoling presence and because we are never as faithful as we should be. God is always partially obscure and we are always partially blind.

It is not my purpose here to debate whether our present experience of God is weak because God is leading us to a deeper level of faith or because there is something not fully right with us. It is always a bit of both, but I want to focus on the latter. I choose this route not because I feel that the conservative thesis is more valid than the liberal one, but because we cannot, in the end, do anything about God's freedom, about whether God chooses to give us dark nights of the soul. We can, however, do something about our disposition towards God. Our focus will be on our struggles in faith insofar as they constitute a fault on our part, a fault that can be mended.

What is less than perfect within us that dulls and muddies our experience of God? If each age is unique in its unhappiness, what is at the root of our own age's unhappy religious struggle?

The struggle to experience God is not so much one of God's presence or absence as it is one of the presence or absence of God *in our awareness*. God is always present, but we are not always present to God. As one spiritual writer put it, "God is no more present in a church than in a drinking bar, but, generally, we are more present to God in a church than in a bar."[6]

Jesus says, "Blessed are the pure of heart for they shall see God."[7] Awareness of God is tied to a certain state of mind and heart, namely, purity. Classical spiritual writers have always identified purity of heart with contemplation. The struggle to purify consciousness through contemplation so as to better experience God is the struggle for a fuller awareness. In Western culture today, most of us have an atrophied contemplative faculty, a muddied self-awareness. God is present to us, but we are not present to God. We lack the ability to be contemplative, and because of this we lack a vital experience of God. The eclipse of God in ordinary awareness is a fault in contemplation. What does this mean?

The Eclipse of God
as a Fault in Contemplation

How is our self-awareness muddied? How do we lack purity of heart?

Experience has shades of quality, degrees of openness. We are aware and awake according to more or less. God can be very present in an event but we can be so preoccupied and focused on our headaches, heartaches, tasks, daydreams, and distracting restlessness that we can be oblivious to that presence.

These things severely limit our awareness. Normally there is a huge gap between what we are aware of and what is available for us to be aware of. The quality and depth of our ordinary experience in general determine our awareness or non-awareness of God. We can be asleep or awake to where God appears. Our awareness in ordinary life, or lack of it, depends upon our ability to be contemplative.

═════════════ ◊ ═════════════

If each age is unique in its unhappiness,
what is at the root of our own age's
unhappy religious experience?

Contemplation is about waking up. To be contemplative is to experience an event fully, in all its aspects. Biblically this is expressed as coming "face to face" with God, others and the cosmos.[8] We are in contemplation when we stand before reality and experience it without the limits and distortions that are created by narcissism (our headaches and heartaches), pragmatism (our pressing tasks), and excessive restlessness (our dreams and distractions).

Spiritual writers like St. John of the Cross assure us that if our awareness is not reduced or distorted, there will be present in ordinary experience a sense of the infinite, the sacred, God. If we are fully awake to ordinary experience, it brings with it a certain *contuition* of God.[9] If our ordinary awareness is diminished, if it is not contemplative, God dies in our awareness and eventually in our churches as well.

Our struggle with unbelief, the struggle to make God more real in ordinary life, is really a struggle with contemplation. But are we not natural contemplatives? Hasn't the study of psychology and the social sciences given us deeper self-understanding? Do we not, today more than ever before, crave solitude, peace, and quiet?

All those things are true. But none of these necessarily mean that we are contemplative in our daily lives. It is obvious is that our sense of God is weak. This can only mean that our contemplative sense is likewise weak. Why is this so?

It is tempting to be unduly negative or, alternately, unduly uncritical of our culture. We tend to be optimists or pessimists, liberals or conservatives, by temperament and, accordingly, it is easy to be overly generous or overly critical in assessing any situation. In assessing our culture we must first point out its ambivalence. It has its strengths and its weaknesses, which are often the shadow sides of its strengths. However, it is clear that interiority and contemplation are not its strengths. Theologian Jan Walgrave once commented that "our age constitutes a virtual conspiracy against the interior life."[10]

It is, of course, not a deliberate conspiracy, deviously and consciously designed by some group with a vested interest in destroying values. But an accidental confluence of historical circumstances, a convergence of accidents now meeting in Western history, make it harder for us to live the examined life.

What forces conspire against the interior life? A rather simplistic view all too common today submits that today's faith struggles have their roots in the social changes of the 1960s. Rock music, the Beatles, the Vietnam war, drugs, the sexual revolution, affluence, the emergence of the first post-rags-to-riches generation, new technologies, and new opportunities for travel and anonymity, it suggests, changed our conception of family, marriage, morality, God and religion. Life in the Western world changed rather fundamentally in the last three decades and, with that change, the old ideals of family and religion were undermined. Problems with faith today, according to this view, are rooted in the social changes that occurred in the last generation.

This is an oversimplification. When Nietzsche's madman smashes his lantern and shouts: "God is dead and we are his murderers!" the process that he refers to has taken place over many centuries. A generation that feels that God is dead is at the end of a long historical process that killed God unknowingly, gradually, and imperceptibly, often with the very means it was employing to keep him alive.[11] The present crisis has roots that reach back hundreds of years.[12]

The reason why our generation struggles with a certain practical atheism has its roots in changes that began in Western history with the birth of the Renaissance and the advent of modern science and modern philosophy. A seed was planted then which has only come to full bloom in the latter part of the twentieth century.

Notes

1. Leo Tolstoy, *Anna Karenina*. Pt. i, chap. I. Translation by Maude.

2. Friedrich Nietzsche, *The Gay Science*, ET. W. Kaufmann (New York: Vintage Books, 1974), p. 167.

3. Philip Rieff, *The Triumph of the Therapeutic* (New York: Harper Torchbooks, 1966).

4. This and the subsequent quotations in this paragraph are taken from F. Nietzsche, *The Gay Science*. Book 3, no. 125, the edition cited above, p. 182.

5. John of the Cross, *The Living Flame of Love*. Commentary on Stanza 3, numbers 70–76, translated by K. Kavanaugh and O. Rodriguez. ICS Publications (Washington, D.C., 1979), pp. 637–40.

6. Sheila Cassidy, *Prayer for Pilgrims* (London, 1980), p. 61.

7. Matthew 5:8.

8. 1 Corinthians 13:12-13. This definition of contemplation is used by many of the classical writers on spirituality, e.g., John of the Cross.

9. The term *contuition* was originally coined by a Benedictine monk of Stanbrook (who published under that name), in *Medieval Mystical Tradition and John of the Cross* (London, 1954), p. 70. Austin Farrer uses it in his philosophical essay *Finite and Infinite: A Philosophical Essay* (Westminster, 1943). Farrer says that *within ordinary perception,* if ordinary perception is fully open to all the dimensions of reality, one perceives ("contuits"), *alongside* the finite, the infinite. Hence, it is not exactly synonymous with the term *intuition.* In intuition something is grasped beyond what is strictly warranted by perception and the logical reasoning processes that follow upon perception. In contuition insight goes beyond strict sense perception, but this insight is had *alongside* and *as part of* ordinary sense perception and, consequently, is warranted by ordinary perception. It is the contemplative dimension of perception.

10. In private conversation, expanded into a short article (see Ronald Rolheiser, "Just Too Busy to Bow Down," in *Forgotten among the Lilies* [London: Hodder & Stoughton, 1990], pp. 12–114).

11. We often kill God by bad religion. Atheism, though, is most often generated by bad theism. Michael Buckley discusses this in his monumental *At the Origins of Modern Atheism* (New Haven: Yale University Press, 1987).

12. For an analysis of those historical roots, see Ronald Rolheiser, "The Deeper Causes Underlying Our Present Difficulties in Believing," *Louvain Studies* (1994).

two

Narcissism, Pragmatism, Unbridled Restlessness, and the Non-Contemplative Personality

Factors Militating Against Contemplation

Jesus promised that if we have purity of heart, we shall see God. What blocks this purity of heart? If God is there to be experienced, why is He not more compelling in our experience? Why do we so often confuse the experience of God with our own projects and self-interests? Why is our awareness not more open and less obtuse?

Narcissism

Prior to the birth of philosophy, ancient Greece crystallized much of its religious and psychological wisdom into a series of myths. One such myth is that of Narcissus.

Narcissus was the son of the river god, Cephissus, and a youth of surpassing beauty and vanity. A mountain nymph, Echo, fell in love with him, but he was cold to her. Eventually she pined away to only a voice, because her love for him found no response. Because of this, the god Nemesis determined to punish Narcissus for his vanity. He caused him to go for a drink at a pool of water. When he saw his reflection, Narcissus was overcome with his own beauty; he fell in love with himself. Turned inward and paralyzed by his obsession with himself, he eventually withered away and became a flower that still bears his name.

Freudian psychology uses this name as the technical term in psychoanalysis for excessive self-preoccupation—narcissism.

Few images provide as apt a description of the contemporary mindset. If we are not a generation in love with itself, we are, undeniably, one that is obsessed with itself.

We see this narcissism, first of all, in our propensity for individualism and our corresponding inability to be healthily aware of and concerned about the reality beyond our private lives. To offer a simple but clear illustration: For the past some years, I have been involved in a marriage preparation course. This course is a requirement for marriage in various churches. Many who attend are not there out of their own choice. In our sessions, we do battle with their many objections, which rarely deal with the substance of what is being discussed—the nature of marriage. Rather, the primary (often hostile) objection is to the idea of the course itself: "Why do we have to take this course? Why are the church and society concerned about *my* marriage? *My* marriage is nobody's business. This is *my* life, *my* love, *my* sex, *my* honeymoon, *my* future, *my* concern!"

People who raise these questions and objections betray an individualism, a lack of a sense of the communal, a lack of a sense of reality outside themselves that is seriously unhealthy. One expects to hear objections like this from the children of René Descartes, not from the children of Jesus Christ. The great philosopher, searching for the very first point of his philosophy, questioned the reality of everything until he came to one he could not doubt: *"I think, therefore, I am!"* In Descartes' mind, the one thing we can be sure of, can know is real, is ourselves. We might be dreaming everything else.

The objections of the young people I just quoted echo the lonely voice of Descartes doubting the reality of everything beyond the private world of his own self. What they are really saying is, My heartaches, my headaches, my wounds, my problems, my chronic shortage of money, my mortgage, my tasks, and my worries are real. Other people's lives and the larger community and its concerns are not real."

This type of self-centeredness is not surprising, nor is it unique to our age. The structure of the human personality as a center of self-awareness makes us by nature narcissistic. To ourselves we are always massively real. Our own reality is always the paramount one. Today, however, a conspiracy of accidents has intensified our natural proclivity for self-preoccupation to the point where we are trapped within ourselves.

Narcissism, insofar as it adversely affects contemplation, is characterized by four salient features:

The Incapacity to Recognize the Reality of Others

This characteristic is evident in the example just given. These young people and their objections are the children of our culture, incarnations of its attitudes. In them, we

see the struggle we all have to see that others and the
world outside us are as real as we are.

The Yuppie Instinct
for the Quality of Life

The *yuppie phenomenon* may not sound serious, but the
reality it describes is one of the more significant devel-
opments in recent Western culture.

What is a yuppie?[1]

We guide our lives more by unconscious myth and
feeling than we do by rationality and so we may define
the term yuppie by four interpenetrating slogans: Quality of Life, Upward Mobility, the Pursuit of Excellence,
and Material Comfort.

ᘯ

*Self-development is pursued with a sense
of duty and asceticism that were formerly
reserved for religion.*

The unconscious, and in many cases the conscious,
myth that moves people today is one of success, of moving up the ladder, of being rich, of having a beautiful
body, of being well dressed, of having prestige, of luxuri-
ating in material comfort, of achieving—in comfort—
everything that is potentially attainable. This brings
with it unashamed ambition and the expressed desire to
leave the pack behind. An important part of the quality
of being a yuppie is to set oneself, through excellence,
above others.

Obviously, not all of this is bad, nor novel. People have always wanted these things and the myths of past generations (e.g., rags to riches, work hard and get ahead) hardly seem different. Neither is there anything inherently immoral in these things. The emphasis on excellence should not be challenged. What is novel, less moral, and needs challenge is the fact that it is tied to an explicit philosophy of life in which unbridled individualism, selfishness, and idiosyncratic development are unabashedly held up as virtues. Self-development is salvation pure and simple. Everything—marriage, family, community, justice, church, morality, service to others, sacrifice—makes sense and has value only insofar as it enhances one's self. Self-development is pursued with a sense of duty and asceticism that were formerly reserved for religion because, for the yuppie, self-development *is* salvation, the religious project.

How deeply we are influenced by this ideal is evident in a variety of ways, including what we read and what we admire.

When we survey the non-fiction best-seller lists of recent years, we see that virtually every one of the books on the lists has to do with achievement, the rewards of success, quality of life, and the pursuit of excellence. This is also apparent in the proclivity we have for the rich and the famous. Neil Postman, in *Amusing Ourselves to Death,* describes the 1983 commencement exercises at Yale University. Several honorary doctorates were awarded, including one to Mother Theresa. As she and the others received their degrees, the audience applauded appropriately, but with a slight hint of reserve and impatience, "for it wished to give its heart to the final recipient who waited shyly in the wings." As the details of her achievements were read, many of the audience left their seats and surged toward the stage. When the name of the final recipient—Meryl Streep—was announced, the audience "unleashed a sonic boom of affection, enough to wake the New Haven dead."[2] This is not intended as a criticism of Meryl Streep. She is a fine actress and, by all indications, a fine human being as well. The point is the audience's reaction, one typical of our culture, and one that shows what we value most highly.

Ultimately, this is narcissism, perhaps not as the textbooks lay it out, but certainly of the sort Freud would recognize. We are a culture very much caught up in the idiosyncratic.

The Movement towards
Excessive Privacy

There is a relentless movement towards greater privatization in virtually every area of life. In our culture, the ideal is to have a private car, a private office, a private home; and within that home, a private room, a private bathroom, a private phone, a private stereo system, and a private television set and video recorder.

The movement towards excessive privacy is well-depicted in the image of a shopper in a busy supermarket with headphones on. They pass up the possibility of being potentially social, and move inside their own private world. Speak of receding into oneself!

The law in most of Western culture also reveals this demand for excessive privacy. For most of us, the ideal of law and order is that of the *Pax Romanum*, namely, that

law should maintain enough public order so that everyone can do their own thing. By most standards in the
West, that is the definition of human rights.

There is nothing inherently wrong with privacy. No
one comes to maturity or stays there except through a
healthy balance of social interaction and privacy. What
is at issue is excessiveness. When this need is unchecked,
meaningful social interaction diminishes and the opportunity to escape into a world of private projects, private
dreams, and private fantasies increases. Narcissism
grows stronger when there is not enough meaningful
social interaction to draw us out of our selves and make
us aware of the reality outside us. This movement
towards greater privacy is both a symptom and a cause
of narcissism.

The Inability to Act Out of a Purpose
Beyond the Idiosyncratic Preference

We are so preoccupied with our own inner worlds today
that we find it difficult to act out of any motivation
beyond that of doing our own thing.

Sociologist Robert Bellah gives an excellent example
of this in his fine book *Habits of the Heart*.[3] He recounts
the story of Brian, a young California businessman who
has, in his own mind, changed his value system after the
trauma of a divorce. As a youth, he had given himself to
the pursuit of pleasure, in his own words, to "hell-raising
and sex." Later he married, settled down, assumed a
very responsible job, and fathered three children. His
marriage, while not an unhappy one for him, was not
the focus of his life; his work and career were. He worked

65–70 hours a week and seldom took weekends off. His career skyrocketed and his marriage died. One night he came home to an empty house. His wife had left him.

The divorce was a major shock to him. Unaccustomed to failure of any kind, the demise of his marriage provoked a crisis that eventually led him to radically alter his priorities. When he finally remarried, marriage and family life was something different to him; the primary thing in his life is his family. When something has to be sacrificed, it is the job that gets shortchanged. Brian is happy and has a new sense of energy and enthusiasm, which he attributes to his family and his new priorities.

When we stand before reality preoccupied with ourselves we will see precious little of what is actually there to be seen.

In many ways, this sounds like a conversion story. The difficulty arises, as Bellah points out, when Brian tries to explain why his present life is better than his former one. In the end, his reasons for what he is now doing, and his belief in its worth, are little different from his reasons for pursuing pleasure as an adolescent and business success as a younger adult—it makes him feel good. He did his thing then, and he is still doing his thing now.

An outsider might point out that, in terms of the overall picture, the collective social structure, his present lifestyle and values are more beneficial to the whole than was his past. But that was not his reason for changing his lifestyle and adjusting his values. In the end, his justification of his present lifestyle is the same as for his past: idiosyncratic preference.

Brian is more typical than deviant in representing our culture in this. For the most part, we, like him, do not connect our values and priorities to a structure of value beyond personal preference and the comfort of our own inner worlds. In the end, our own reality is the only one that is real and important.

How does this adversely affect contemplation? The effect of excessive narcissism on contemplation is simple. When we stand before reality preoccupied with ourselves we will see precious little of what is actually there to be seen. Moreover, what little we do see will be distorted and shaped by self-interest.

Imagine taking a walk in a beautiful forest on a splendid summer's day. The earth is ablaze with the fire of God and the sights, sounds, and smells are enough to make you want to take your shoes off before the burning bush. But if your mind and heart are hopelessly torn, and if, for example, you are painfully infatuated with someone who has just rejected you, you will see virtually nothing on this walk—not just of beauty and creation, but nothing at all. You are inside yourself, torn by your pain, endlessly reviewing past and future conversations, possibilities, and fantasies. For all you are actually seeing, hearing, or smelling of beauty and nature, you could just as profitably be walking in a parking lot or a rubbish dump. You are locked in an inner world whose obsessive reality absorbs all your awareness. The outside world has little power to penetrate or even to distract you. Your reality has been reduced to the size, shape, and color of your own inner world.

The image of an obsessed person walking through a scene of beauty and being oblivious to it illustrates how narcissism is the antithesis of contemplation. It is also an image of our culture's struggle to see God in ordinary life. When we are excessively preoccupied with ourselves, we tend to see nothing beyond our own heartaches and problems and our sense of reality shrinks. It is not surprising that we have trouble believing in the reality of God when we have trouble perceiving any reality at all beyond ourselves.

Pragmatism

Pragmatism is synonymous with Western life, particularly with American life. The word comes from the Greek *pragma,* which means "business," but also has connotations of efficiency, sensibleness, and practicality.

Pragmatism is a philosophy and a way of life that asserts that the truth of an idea lies in its practical efficacy. What that means is that what is true is what works. The test for truth is not whether an idea corresponds to the way things are, but whether the idea has some concrete utility, practical consequences, or can be used to manipulate the world beneficially. Worth lies in achievement. Things are good if they work, and what works is good. The ideals of pragmatism lie at the very heart of the Western mind, undergird our technological society, are deeply enshrined in our educational systems, and are evident in our impatience with anything (or anybody) that is not practical, useful, and efficient.

Much of this, of course, is good. There can be no dispute that many of the things in our modern world that have helped to make life better—medicine, travel, tech-

nological advances, and communications—are largely
the result of a pragmatic approach to life. It is not honest to enjoy the benefits of these things and unquali-
fiedly criticize the philosophy and way of life that
produced them. But it is important to recognize that
pragmatism brings with it some debilitating side-effects.

Taking Our Sense of Worth from
What We Do Rather Than from Who We Are

If we accept the pragmatic principle that what's good is
what works, then you are only good if you work . . . and
you are only as good as the work you do. Those equations wreak havoc in our lives.

Psychologists assure us that happiness depends
largely upon having a healthy self-image. We are happy
when we feel good about ourselves and we are not
happy when we do not. In a pragmatic society, unfortunately, we feel good about ourselves only when we are
achieving, producing, and contributing in a pragmatic
way. We feel good and important when we do things
that society values as good and important and we feel
useless and unimportant when we do things that society
does not value. We hand out admiration and respect on
the basis of pragmatic achievement more than on the
basis of moral virtue or quality of personality. In a pragmatic society *doing* counts for everything, *being* counts
for nothing. We cling to what we do, not who we are, as
if it were life itself.

The effects of this attitude make themselves felt
everywhere: achievement of professional goals takes
precedence over family life, personal virtue, and leisure;
persons who are retired, unemployed, or at home with

children feel unfulfilled and useless; we have no place for handicapped persons, for the aged, for the sick; we end up as part of the rat race—with no time and no leisure, high blood pressure, and a diminished sense of enjoyment—and do not know how we got there or how to get away from it; and, finally, when doing is everything and being is nothing, we end up with nothing to help us prepare for death.

Having Little Patience *for Impractical Ideas*

In a pragmatic world, the purpose of human thought is for problem solving. Ideas are meant to help us adapt more comfortably to a hostile environment. Consequently, we learn as a means, not as an end in the Western world. Education is more about skills for life than about achieving wisdom. Our educational systems, research grants, and the approach we take to learning reflect this priority. We spend more money for research on developing better rubber for our car tires than we spend on studying why teenage suicide is the second leading cause of death among young people today in the Western world. Technology is developing at a rate that staggers our capacity to cope with the novelties it produces and, at the same time, we cannot find ways to live together in our marriages, communities, countries, and the world as a whole. The priorities that a pragmatic culture sets in education are very useful in creating the good life but less useful in providing the values we need to share it equitably and amiably with each other.

Trusting Only the Scientific Method

When the purpose of thought is to be able to manipulate things for the benefit of humanity, then the scientific method takes center stage and, eventually, the whole stage. In a pragmatic society, science alone is given the right to establish facts. Its findings are considered objective. What is proposed by other disciplines with a different method of knowing—metaphysics, philosophy, mysticism, poetry, or theology—is deemed purely subjective, a matter of personal faith. No one, for example, professional scientist or lay person, has ever seen an atom. Yet none of us doubts its existence. Science not only assures us that atoms exist, it manipulates them to create nuclear energy. Who can doubt their existence? Likewise, no one, professional mystic or lay person, has ever seen God in this world. Yet we doubt God's existence—despite the fact that mystics assure us of His reality and we see in the lives of believers (not to mention Christ, Buddha, and Mohammed) concrete evidence that they are experiencing something real in what they call an experience of God. They, too, like the scientists, are splitting atoms that release energy. But in a technological society, we see and understand only one kind of energy—practical. This is a debilitating impoverishment that reduces our contemplative abilities.

Thomas Merton was once asked by a journalist what he considered to be the leading spiritual disease of our time. His answer surprised his interviewer. Of all the things he might have suggested (lack of prayer, lack of community, poor morals, lack of concern for justice and the poor) he answered instead with one word: efficiency. Why? Because, "from the monastery to the

Pentagon, the plant has to run . . . and there is little time or energy left over after that to do anything else." Merton is pointing out that, when it comes to God and religion, our problem is not so much badness as it is busyness. We are not very contemplative, he's saying, because the demands of our lives absorb all of our energies and time.

A 1989 *Time Magazine* cover story entitled "The Rat Race: How America Is Running Itself Ragged"[4] pointed out that time has become the most precious commodity in today's world, that parents have to make appointments to spend time with their own children, that technology has increased the very heartbeat of today's generation, that for many persons the demands of staying on top of their careers take all their time and energy. How much worse things have grown in the ensuing decade! In our world, there is simply no time or energy (or even the capacity) to pray or be contemplative. The expression "caught in the rat race" says it all. As the *Time* article puts it, "with too little time for sleep there is also too little time for dreams."

There is a more subtle manner in which pragmatism works against contemplation. When self-worth depends on achievement, then very few persons are going to spend much time in prayer or contemplation since these are by definition not utilitarian efforts. They are useless in a practical manner, a waste of time. Contemplation and prayer do not accomplish anything, produce anything, or add anything concrete to life. We feel better about ourselves when we are doing useful things. We have little time for what is useless and, for that, we are contemplatively the poorer. Caught up as we are in the efficiency demanded by our culture, we often end up like the people in Christ's parable who refused the king's invitation to the wedding banquet.[5] They did not turn down the invitation explicitly at all; they simply never showed up. They were too busy.

Unbridled Restlessness

We are a restless people.

Restlessness is the opposite of being restful. Restfulness is one of the most primal cravings humans have. We crave rest to the point where we identify it with heaven: "Grant us eternal rest."

We feel better about ourselves when we are doing useful things. We have little time for what is useless and, for that, we are contemplatively the poorer.

Today, as our lives grow more pressured, as we grow more tired, as we begin to feel burned out, we fantasize more about restfulness. We imagine a peaceful, quiet place: we see ourselves walking by a lake, watching a peaceful sunset, smoking a pipe in a rocker by the fireplace. But even in those images, we make restfulness yet another activity, something we do, something we are refreshed by . . . then we return to normal life.

True restfulness, though, is a form of awareness, a way of being in life. It is living ordinary life with a sense of ease, gratitude, appreciation, peace, and prayer. We are restful when ordinary life is enough.

Thomas Merton, in a journal written during an extended period of solitude, wrote:

> It is enough to be, in an ordinary human mode, with one's hunger and sleep, one's cold and warmth, rising and going to bed. Putting on blankets and taking them off, making coffee and then drinking it. Defrosting the refrigerator, reading, meditating, working, praying, I live as my fathers have lived on this earth, until eventually I die. Amen. There is no need to make an assertion of my life, especially so about it as mine, though doubt less it is not somebody else's. I must learn gradually to forget program and artifice.[6]

Today, nothing seems enough for us. The simple and primal joys of living, those Merton describes, are lost as we grow ever more restless, driven, compulsive, and hyper. There is less ease in our lives, and more fever; less peacefulness, and more obsessive activity; less enjoyment, and more excess. These are the signs of unbridled restlessness.

Have we not always been restless? Are we not pilgrims on earth, built with hearts made for the infinite, yet caught up in very finite and limited lives? Should we be surprised that we are constantly tormented by the insufficiency of everything attainable? To be hopelessly restless proves little more than that we are alive, emotionally healthy, and normal. Has not God built us so that we are restless until we rest in God?

Yes. Restlessness is normal. However, it is like body temperature; beyond a point it becomes an unhealthy fever. Our psychic temperature today has risen to become such a pitch. Our restlessness is excessive. A healthy restlessness pushes us to be dissatisfied with the limits of this life, but restlessness becomes unhealthy when, as Merton puts it, it is "no longer enough to be in an ordinary human mode."

Our restlessness is pushing us beyond what is healthy. Three related factors impact adversely on our ability to be contemplative:

Greed for Experience

When restlessness is excessive it is no longer possible to be satisfied with being just a human being ("with one's own hunger and sleep . . . cold and warmth . . . making coffee and drinking it"). What is simple and primal, the feel of one's own body and the taste of one's own coffee, is lost in an obsessive greed for experience.

Scholastic philosophy used to say that the adequate object of human yearning is all being insofar as it is knowable and good. That is a rather abstract way of saying that what would ultimately satisfy us would be to experience everybody and everything and be experienced by everyone and everything. Our bodies, minds, and hearts are greedy for experience.

When restlessness becomes excessive, this greed for experience, which normally underlies and motivates all of our actions in a positive way, begins to drive us outward so that our actions do not issue forth from some free center, but from compulsion. Our lives become consumed with the idea that unless we somehow experience everything, travel everywhere, see everything, and are part of a large number of other people's experience, then we are small and meaningless. We are impatient with every hunger, every ache, and every non-consummated area within our lives; we are convinced that unless every pleasure we yearn for is tasted, we will be unhappy.

In this posture of unbridled restlessness, we stand before life too greedy, too full of expectations that cannot be realized, and unable to accept that, here, in this life, all symphonies remain unfinished. We are unable to rest or be satisfied because we are convinced that all lack, all tension, and all unfulfilled yearning is tragic. Thus, it is tragic to be alone, to be unmarried, to be married but not completely fulfilled romantically and sexually; not to be good looking or to be unhealthy, aged, or handicapped. It is tragic to be caught up in duties and commitments that limit our freedom, tragic to be poor, tragic to go through life without tasting every pleasure and fulfilling every potential inside us.

When we are obsessed in this way it is hard to be contemplative. We are too focused on our own heartaches to be open and receptive.

Impatience and Lack of Chastity

Some years ago, before the demise of communism in the Soviet Union, I was involved in a bizarre incident that helped highlight for me our culture's struggle with patience. I was journeying to the U.S.S.R. with a group of Western tourists. We arrived in Moscow on a snowy December evening, cleared customs, and moved toward our connecting flight to St. Petersburg. Then, for reasons never explained to us, we were made to wait . . . for twenty-four hours.

Hundreds of other people also waited in the airport that night. Only our group, the Westerners, appeared to be in a panic. We rushed from desk to desk, demanding explanations and phoning embassies. Blood pressures and temperatures ran high and there was the constant expression of indignation: "Nobody can do this to us! We don't have to put up with this!"

What was enlightening about this event was that it was soon clear who in that airport was from the West and who was not. We were angry, impatient, and contemptuous. The Eastern Europeans, on the other hand, waited passively. They smoked, played cards, and drank vodka. Obviously, they were used to waiting. A day later, our flight to St. Petersburg was announced and our vigil was over. Except that it had not been a vigil. From beginning to end, we had fought the waiting and seen it as an imposition on our rights. Later, in a more reflective moment, I was able to see in this incident an important lesson.

Just as we rushed around that airport convinced that nobody or nothing had a right to deny us what we wanted, so too we rush about our lives refusing to wait for things, refusing to live in any tension, convinced that nobody or nothing has a right to deny us what we want.

We see the effect of this impatience in our economics, in our sexual morality, and in our constant tendency to seize, as by right, what is by nature a gift. There is in our culture an inability to wait and, in this, a lack of chastity that is severely debilitating to contemplation.

Chastity is normally defined as having to do with sex, namely, a certain innocence, purity, discipline, or even celibacy. This definition is too narrow. Chastity is not primarily a sexual concept. It has to do with the limits and appropriateness of all experience, the sexual included. To be chaste means to experience all things respectfully and to drink them in only when we are ready for them. We break chastity when we experience anything irreverently or prematurely. All irreverence and prematurity violate chastity.

Experience can be good or bad. It can glue the psyche together or tear it apart. It can produce joy or chaos. Travel, reading, achievement, sex, exposure to novelty, the breaking of taboos, all can be good, if experienced reverently and at their proper time. Conversely, they can tear the soul apart (even when they are not wrong in themselves) when they are not experienced chastely, that is, when they are experienced in a way that does not fully respect the other person or object that is the subject of the experience, or that does not respect our own integration.

Unbridled restlessness makes us unhealthily impatient for experience. Greed and impatience push us towards premature and irresponsible experience, sometimes in very subtle ways. We do a lot of things that are very innocent in themselves, but which, in the end, violate chastity. For example, we give in to our children's demands and allow them everything they demand—travel at a very young age, every kind of consumer object, exposure to whatever movies and videos they desire, dating at age twelve, sex at age sixteen—and then we wonder why they are bored, cynical, and fatigued in spirit at age twenty.

Allan Bloom submits that lack of patience and chastity leads to "an eros gone lame." Speaking not from any particular religious perspective but solely from that of a humanist and educator, he asserts that we are born for a high purpose. We are also built for that purpose. We are fired into life with a madness that comes from our incompleteness and lets us believe that we can recover our wholeness through the embrace of another, the perpetuity of our seed, and the contemplation of God. According to Bloom we have trivialized this longing and made it mean something more concrete, something small, something less. For us, the longing is now simply for success, pleasure, the sweetening of life. He quotes Plato, who in his *Symposium* tells how his students sit around "telling wonderful stories of the meaning of their immortal longings." Bloom points out how his own students sit around and tell less wonderful stories of sexual yearnings much more concretely channeled.[7]

At the root of this, says Bloom, lies the lack of chastity. Speaking outside any consideration of Christian morality, he suggests that it is premature and non-integrative sexual experience that is lobotomizing today's soul and dulling its eros. Premature experience, he asserts, is bad precisely because it is premature. The period of nascent yearning is meant for sublimation—in the sense of making sublime, of orientating youthful inclinations and longings towards great love, great art, great achievement. Premature experience is like the false ecstasy of drugs in that "it artificially induces the exaltation naturally attached to the completion of the greatest endeavors—victory in a just war, consummated love, artistic creation, religious devotion, and the discovery of truth."[8] It has the effect of draining great enthusiasm and great expectations that can only be built up through sublimation, tension, and waiting.

Bloom says that in his experience as a teacher he finds that students who have had a serious fling with drugs—and got over it—find it difficult to have enthusiasm and great expectations: "it is as though the color has been drained out of their lives and they see everything in black and white. . . . They function perfectly well, but dryly, routinely. Their energy has been sapped, and they do not expect their life's activity to produce anything but a living."[9]

A generation earlier, Albert Camus had written, "Chastity alone is connected with personal progress. There is a time when moving beyond it is a victory— when it is released from its moral imperatives. But this quickly becomes defeat afterwards."[10]

Few things work as militantly against contemplation as do impatience and the lack of chastity it invariably spawns. In fact, patience and chastity are, in themselves, almost a definition of contemplation. The perception and reception of God, as is evident in the teaching of the incarnation, are linked to an experience of advent—a period of waiting in tension and living in chastity so as to let God be God and love be gift.

The Loss of Interiority

Socrates once commented that "the unexamined life is not worth living." We have taken to examining our lives less and less.

Distraction is normal in our culture. Contemplativeness, solitude, and prayer are not. Why is this? We are not, either by choice or ideology, a culture set against the interior life. Nor are we, I submit, more afraid of the interior life than people in past ages. Where we differ from past ages is in our busyness and in the degree of our restlessness.

Henri Nouwen describes our contemporary lives:

One of the most obvious characteristics of our daily lives is that we are busy. We experience our days as filled with things to do, people to meet, projects to finish, letters to write, calls to make, and appointments to keep. Our lives often seem like over-packed suitcases bursting at the seams. In fact, we are almost always aware of being behind schedule. There is a nagging sense that there are unfinished tasks, unfulfilled promises, unrealized proposals. There is always something else that we should have remembered, done, or said. There are always people we did not speak to, write to, or visit. Thus, although we are very busy, we have a lingering feeling of never really fulfilling our obligations. . . .

✺

Distraction is normal in our culture.
Contemplativeness, solitude, and prayer are not.

Beneath our worrying lives, however, something else is going on. While our minds and hearts are filled with many things, and we wonder how we can live up to the expectations imposed upon us by ourselves and others, we have a deep sense of unfulfillment. While busy with and worried about many things, we seldom feel truly satisfied, at peace, at home. A gnawing sense of being unfulfilled underlies our filled lives. . . . The great paradox of our time is that many of us are busy and bored at the same time.

> While running from one event to the next, we
> wonder in our innermost selves if anything is
> really happening. While we can hardly keep up
> with our many tasks and obligations, we are not
> so sure that it would make any difference if we
> did nothing at all. While people keep pushing us
> in all directions, we doubt if anyone really cares.
> In short, while our lives are full, we are unful-
> filled.[11]

Being filled yet unfulfilled comes from being without
deep interiority. When there is never time or space to
stand behind our own lives and look reflectively at
them, then the pressures and distractions of life simply
consume us, until we lose control over our lives.

This lack of interiority is largely the product of undis-
ciplined restlessness. When we are unreflective, invariably it is because our restlessness lacks a proper
asceticism and propels us into a flurry of activity that
keeps us preoccupied and consumed with the surface of
life—with the business of making a living, with doing
things, and entertaining ourselves. It is then that our
actions no longer issue from a center within us, but
instead are products of compulsion. We do things and
we no longer know why. We feel chronically pressured,
victimized, and hyper-driven. We overwork, but are
bored; socialize excessively, but are lonely; work to the
point of exhaustion, but feel like our lives are a waste.

This is the unexamined life as Socrates spoke of it. It
is also at the heart of Greek mythology's *Myth of Sisyphus.* Sisyphus was a man condemned, for no good reason, to roll a stone up a hill forever. As soon as he got it
to the top it rolled back down again, and he had to
return to the bottom and roll it back up. This is an

image of frustration, of futilely having to do an activity which one is powerless to stop. It is also an image of the fruits of a non-contemplative life.

Restlessness without proper reflection destroys contemplation and, with it, the sense of God within ordinary life. Why? Because when we operate out of restlessness rather than out of our true center, then, in the famous phrase of Augustine, God is within us, but we are outside of ourselves.[12]

"Blessed are the pure of heart, for they shall see God." What makes our hearts less than pure? It is not always simply sin, moral laxity, or bad will. Narcissism, pragmatism, and excessive restlessness can effectively block us from seeing God in ordinary life.

Notes

1. The term *yuppie* stands for Young Urban Professionals.

2. Neil Postman, *Amusing Ourselves to Death: Public Discourse in the Age of Show Business* (New York: Penguin Books, 1985), pp. 96–97.

3. Robert Bellah, Richard Madsen, William Sullivan, Ann Swidler, and Steven Tipton, *Habits of the Heart: Individualism and Commitment in American Life* (San Francisco: Harper and Row, 1985), pp. 3–6.

4. Marguerite Michaels and James Willwerth, "How America Has Run Out of Time," in *Time Magazine,* 24 April 1989, pp. 48–55.

5. Luke 14:16-24 and Matthew 22:1-14.

6. Quoted by John Howard Griffin, *Follow the Ecstasy* (Fort Worth Tex.: JHG Editions, Latitudes Press, 1983), pp. 37–38.

7. Allan Bloom, *The Closing of the American Mind* (New York: Simon and Schuster, 1987), pp. 132–33.

8. *The Closing of the American Mind,* pp. 79–80.

9. Idem.

10. Albert Camus, "A Writer's Notebook," in *Encounter,* volume 24, no. 3 (March 1965), pp. 28–29.

11. Henri Nouwen, *Making All Things New: An Introduction to the Spiritual Life* (New York: Doubleday, 1981), pp. 23–24.

12. Augustine, *The Confessions of St. Augustine,* 10.27.

three

A Radically Changed Situation

The Non-Contemplative Personality

A new personality is emerging in the West. This non-contemplative personality, to a large extent novel in history, is typified by salient qualities that stand in stark contrast to the past:

For the non-contemplative, reality holds no dimensions of mystery beyond the empirical, which is the basis of all that is considered valid within human experience. People no longer expect to discover to discover dimensions of reality beyond the empirically evident. For most of us, the final spiritual exorcism has already taken place. There are no longer any supernatural dimensions to reality, or, in many cases, even to religion. We no longer see spirit lurking within matter, nor the natural world camouflaging the supernatural.

Today's non-contemplative person is not haunted by the scent of unseen roses. The average person today does not ask the old metaphysical question: "Why is there something instead of nothing?" Reality is simply there, something one takes for granted. Reality is the empirical—what can be experienced through the senses—and this needs no explanation beyond its immediate causal nexus. People of the past saw an infinite background to any reality or event; people today see reality against a very concrete, immediate, and pragmatic horizon.

Moreover, people of the past were able to look at reality and experience *wonder;* people today experience only the pragmatic dimension of life. Non-utilitarian purposes are rarely sought in reality.

For today's non-contemplative person reality is, in Bertrand Russell's words, "just there, and that's all!" It is a given. It contains no mysteries beyond its empirical ones.

———————————— ❦ ————————————

For most of us, the final spiritual exorcism has already taken place. There are no longer any supernatural dimensions to reality, or, in many cases, even to religion.

For the non-contemplative nothing is sacrosanct. The non-contemplative believes that there are no sacred taboos. Unlike past generations, who believed that "the fear of the Lord is the beginning of wisdom," the non-contemplative believes that the exorcism of fear of the sacred is the true path to knowledge.

Past generations placed a premium on virginity, on a cautiousness and chastity in experience. They believed that there was a certain authority within the very contours of reality that was not to be violated. Thus, some dimensions of reality carried a mystique (in the deepest sense of that word) that was not to be rendered familiar by indiscriminate experience.

That concept smacks of timidity, ignorance, and naivete today. The non-contemplative person values experience above all. There are no taboos inherent in the nature of things themselves; nor are there mysteries, except those that are the result of lack of knowledge or opportunity to experience. Reality has been stripped of its mystique, rendered familiar, and seen to possess no dimensions before which human beings must show reverence and respect. There is an innocence in the contemplative, and a sophistication that borders on cynical in today's non-contemplative. The path to truth lies in a rigorous examination, in empirical tasting free of all taboos and hesitations that stem from a sense of sacredness or from a fear of violating reality's natural contours as if what can be known can only be known empirically because there is no other sacred dimension.

Naked empirical examination deflates mystery and exorcises the sense of the sacred, which is seen as a superstition born of fear.

For past generations, Adam and Eve's eating of the apple (desirable "for the knowledge it would bring") was seen as a violation of the sacred and as a move antithetical to true knowledge. For today's non-contemplative, the violation of a sacred taboo is the beginning of true wisdom. Consequently, these two types view the connection between morality and epistemology differently.

For the contemplative person the equation was formulated this way: all moral self-centeredness impedes our ability to know properly. Selfishness, self-indulgence, and lack of chastity and reverence in experiencing block purity of heart and distort truth. Therefore, one should be cautious, reticent, and somewhat scrupulous about what taboos one breaks.

For today's non-contemplative indiscriminate experiential testing (and tasting) has replaced chastity, caution, repression, and sublimation as the route to true knowledge. Moreover, scientific analysis has replaced the moral absolutes of Christianity and natural law as the monitor and purifier of awareness. The fear today is not that one might distort experience by being unchaste, but that one might miss out on an experience by being uptight. Where past generations feared that lack of chastity would lead to darkening of the mind, the present generation fears that a lack of nerve to experience anything and everything will leave one with an infantile level of insight.

For the non-contemplative human metaphysics is the final solution and agnosticism has definite limits. The contemplative believes that, since God is radically and totally other than ourselves and our reality, we can live patiently and believe in God, despite seemingly unanswerable paradoxes, and despite pain and injustice. Today's non-contemplative believes that, since there are inexplicable paradoxes, non-vindicated injustices, and unanswerable questions in our present framework, there can be no God. . . . Or if there is, God is less than omnipotent and his metaphysics is similar to ours.

For the contemplative, God's ways are not our ways, his thoughts are not our thoughts. There are two sets of rules for reality, one for the infinite (God) and another for the finite (us). It is understood that the human mind cannot answer questions about things like evil, predestination, or injustice because it is finite and operates with a finite system of symbols. It is by definition limited. Infinite things cannot be grasped by finite minds.

The non-contemplative mind believes, or rather "knows," that there is only one set of rules for reality,

one metaphysics: our own. There is no further framework. Attempts to render a problematic situation intelligible by reference to a higher framework (the *mystery* of
the God) is considered ignorant, superstitious, or cow-
ardly. With this perspective, there is no reason to contemplate because we already know all there is to know.
If there is a God, we know all about him!

So, in opposition to the contemplative whose sense
of mystery allows unlimited questions and answers, the
non-contemplative questions and examines only as far
as known empirical possibilities allow. The agnosticism
of the non-contemplative is limited; the questioning and
wonder end when the empirically verifiable possibilities
are exhausted. The non-contemplative does not live his
life wondering whether his perspective is too narrow
and asphyxiating; he does not grope for dimensions
beyond present metaphysical possibilities. The possibility of wonder is applied only to empirical mysteries like
Einstein's theories. The possibility that there are unseen
roses is *a priori* excluded.

The non-contemplative person has a lower symbolic
hedge. Human beings are distinguished from animals
on the basis of our symbol-making abilities. We make
and use symbols; animals do not. Symbols give our
actions their meaning.

Humans and animals share many common activities. Like us, animals work, live in communities, eat,
play, make love, give birth and take care of their young.
But for us, these things have a far deeper meaning
because we enter them differently and surround them
with symbols. For example, there are two ways a human
being can eat, with symbols or without them.

We often eat without symbols. Eating then is little

different than fueling up a car. We pull up to the table with an empty tank, quickly and non-reflectively gulp down a meal (without tasting our food) and, like a car pulling back onto the road, we leave the table to return to our busy life. We have nourished our bodies.

Or we can eat with symbols. Two people, deeply in love, set out to dine together. They spend time talking before the meal, perhaps having a drink. They approach the carefully laid out table complete with linen cloths, candles, china, and crystal. They hold hands and say a special grace. Then slowly, over the course of hours, they eat. They conclude with a toast and a prayer of thanksgiving. In this case, much more is happening than a simple refueling. The eating has been surrounded with a symbolic hedge, with ritual, mystique, aesthetics, romance, and providence that creates meaning and depth of experience that would be absent without it.

Symbols give meaning to life. We always use them to interpret experience except in our most rote activities. Symbols are not all the same; some open us up to deeper meaning than others. Imagine a middle-aged man who is bothered by chronic back pain. What does this pain mean? It can mean that he has arthritis, a medical symbol; or it can mean he is undergoing some mid-life crisis, a psychological symbol; or it can mean that he is undergoing the paschal mystery, that this is his cross, a religious symbol. Or it might mean all three. The symbols with which we enter and interpret our experience can be low (suffering arthritis) or high (being part of the paschal mystery!).

Unlike the contemplative, the non-contemplative tends to live under what both Philip Rieff and Allan Bloom refer to as a low symbolic hedge.[1] Where the contemplative might refer to his erotic aching as "immortal longings," the non-contemplative is more prone to speak of "being horny"; where the contemplative speaks of "a providential meeting," the non-contemplative is more likely to speak of "an accident"; where the contemplative speaks of finding a "soul mate," the non-contemplative speaks of "great chemistry"; where the contemplative speaks of being "caught up in a painful romance," the non-contemplative is likely to call it "obsessional neurosis"; where the contemplative talks of human restlessness as "a nostalgia for the infinite and a sign of being a pilgrim on earth," the non-contemplative feeling the same discontent will wonder if he needs a career change or a new marriage.

〰️

If the God of the past was too demanding, terrifying, hung up on eternal moral structures and a pre-fab game plan, the God of today is too distant, too uninvolved, too domesticated to merit any adoration.

The non-contemplative considers high symbols illegitimate, naive, and in need of exorcism through realism and analysis. The non-contemplative may concede that deep feelings are real, but any interpretation of their significance that exceeds the sensation itself is rejected. God's apparent absence in ordinary experience is intimately connected to the diminished height of our symbolic hedge.

The non-contemplative person no longer connects the "temple" on earth to the "temple" in heaven. In the word *contemplation* we see the word "temple." This is not an etymological curiosity. Long before it referred to a building on earth, the ancients believed that the word "temple" designated a place in the sky, a certain divine arrangement of the stars, a dwelling for the deities. Part of the root idea of contemplation was to build something on earth something (a building, a personality, a moral structure) which corresponded with the temple in the sky, to bring together the two temples.

Implicit in this idea of contemplation is the concept of obedience; human life must be brought into conformity with a pre-existing divine harmony. Religiously, this was expressed as "the will of God," and the contemplative spent his or her life searching to find and do God's will. The first sin was seen precisely as refusing to kneel to this will. The pious gesture of genuflection captures the implication of this notion of contemplation.

Contemplation as obedience is both foreign and repugnant to the modern personality. There is, for better and for worse, an outright rejection of obedience to a pre-existing will of God, both within church circles and outside them. An understanding of and the practice of genuflection have virtually disappeared, indicating more than a change in ritual piety and liturgical practice. It is not an accident. There is something deeper at stake here. People today are simply less aware of God's presence on a conscious level. It would not occur to them to genuflect. To what? If the God of the past was too demanding, terrifying, hung up on eternal moral structures and a pre-fab game plan, the God of today is too distant, too uninvolved, too domesticated to merit any adoration.

To the extent that God appears at all in the consciousness of the non-contemplative, he does not demand genuflection, nor does he ask that one try to build on earth a temple that matches the one in heaven.

The non-contemplative is work oriented and too busy to go to the wedding banquet. In the scriptural parable of the wedding banquet, the people who were initially invited to the feast missed the banquet. They were too preoccupied with measuring land, testing oxen, and going on honeymoons to take notice of the ongoing feast.

This parable is Jesus's own metaphor for non-contemplative lack of awareness. When life is dominated by the headaches, pressures, and concerns for making a living, running a household, meeting schedules, and measuring up to the demands of an achievement-orientated culture, there is a constant press to manipulate rather than just wonder at the world. When manipulation of reality replaces wonder, there is by definition a reduced awareness. The preoccupation with measuring land and testing oxen reduces the chances of being aware that there is a divinely initiated banquet going on at the heart of ordinary life.

One could answer Nietzsche that a pragmatically-oriented consciousness helped sponge away a good part of our horizon.

For the non-contemplative ordinary awareness is distorted by an unhealthy idiosyncrasy. Western consciousness today is excessively narcissistic. Modern man seems incapable of motivation beyond what pleases us. Narcissistic heartaches and obsessions become a filter through which we see reality, reducing reality to a mirror of our own ego and its needs. The wonder and the gaze of admiration give way to distortion and manipulation.

In *A Portrait of the Artist as a Young Man,* James Joyce powerfully depicts the difference between the gaze of sheer admiration that marks contemplative, aesthetic awareness and the gaze of narcissism that marks distorted and lustful awareness. He describes a young man walking down a beach and seeing a very beautiful, partially clad young girl bathing in the sea. Initially the man's reaction is typical of a hormonally charged male: he ducks into the rocks to get a good look. But he has an extraordinary experience. Instead of feeling lust, he is aware only of this girl's absolute beauty. He simply gazes and admires. There is no longing to possess her, there are no sexual fantasies, there is only awe at beauty.

Narcissism also reduces awareness by falsely enhancing our perception of ourselves as individuals to the point that we incorrectly perceive ourselves as *independent* when in reality we are radically and organically *interdependent* with others and the world. The non-contemplative person experiences little sense of the whole, of our radical connectedness (as elucidated in Bell's theorem[2]), of reality as being somehow all of a piece, of the Body of Christ.

Consequently, a sense of God as a real presence has been elbowed out of consciousness. To the extent that God is given any place at all in human awareness, that place is limited and specific, namely, in our churches and in explicit religious activity. With some effort, we can make ourselves aware of God's presence, but there is no longer a spontaneous contuition of God in everyday life.

Commentators have employed various metaphors to describe this condition: the eclipse of God, the silence of God, living in God's shadow, religion as nostalgia, God as a guilt neurosis, faith as lack of nerve, religion as a universal obsessional neurosis.[3] These metaphors, whether they are proposed by atheists explaining why some remnants of belief still exist or by believers suggesting why our experience of God is so limited, all express one thing—that God is not vital in ordinary experience. God *is* dead in ordinary consciousness. He lives on the fringes—in our churches—but even there, his days are numbered.

This is true not because God does not exist to be experienced, but because we in Western culture have a very reduced experience of God. God is present to us, but we are no longer present to God because we are no longer contemplative. Our contemplative faculty—like a limb that has been immobilized in a cast and is now healed and healthy but unable to function without rehabilitation—needs exercise and therapy. Or, like a weightlifter who has overdeveloped certain muscles to the detriment of others and has distorted his natural body, we have overfocused on one part of our consciousness and neglected another to the point where our natural consciousness is distorted.

We are living the unexamined life, and its price is a practical atheism. Fortunately, it can be overcome by contemplative awareness. God will be seen in ordinary experience when ordinary experience is fully open to him.

Contemplation has four major connotations: it implies an experiential knowledge, direct contact with someone or something, a form of obedience, of bringing one's life into conformity with God, and an experience of reality that is not reduced, distorted, or manipulated through narcissism or pragmatism.[4] It is seeing face to face, without the "glass, reflecting darkly."[5]

Tertullian once said: "If I give you a rose you will not doubt God any more, but, of course, the rose has to unlock a mystical insight and appreciation."[6] When we perceive reality in a non-practical, non-controlling, and admiring way, we are being contemplative. When reality is allowed to be all that it is and the human mind is allowed to experience it as it is, we know the scent of unseen roses; the aesthetic, religious, poetic, romantic, ironic, and humorous dimensions of ordinary reality leap to the fore.

God will be seen in ordinary experience when
ordinary experience is fully open to him.

There is a fundamental shift in our attitude towards reality when we perceive it contemplatively. From wondering *how* and wondering *whether,* we begin a wondering *at.* The door to the invisible begins to open and we sense a previously unperceived depth within ordinary reality. In this attitude, a contuition of God in ordinary experience is not only possible, it is natural and spontaneous, and it changes us.

Contemplation also brings about union with God, others, and the cosmic world. Meeting and experiencing the presence of the other radically changes the person entering into it. Classical spiritualities already know that all contemplation purifies, purges, and enlarges the subject entering into it. Contemporary spiritualities, drawing on new insights taken from psychology and sociology, corroborate this.

Contemplation is genuine union with others and the experience of unity helps break unhealthy narcissism. It becomes a light that shows us our idiosyncrasies, our fantasies, our dishonesties, and our selfishness. In this way, contemplation cuts the roots of our sin. Genuine union is incompatible with dishonesty, fantasy, and self-ishness. It is why classical spiritual writers state that contemplation is always a very painful experience.

Contemplation is not something we must learn, but something we must relearn, and relearn again, throughout our lives.

In some Eastern religions, radical union within community (divine, human, cosmic) is understood as swallowing up individual subjectivity. Contemplation, as is understood in the Western Christian tradition, suggests the opposite. Far from limiting or eliminating individual self-consciousness, contemplative union (and all other genuine unity) enhances it. As recent sociology and psychology agree, individuality is not incompatible with communion but dependent upon it. Conversely, lack of community eventually destroys self-identity. Contemplation, therefore, also deepens self-awareness.

Since contemplation changes wondering *how* to wondering *at,* it brings forth the sheer enjoyment of beauty without the urge to possess it, manipulate it, or assimilate it, dampening the pragmatic urge.

A child is a natural contemplative, constantly wondering *at*. Everything is laden with aesthetic and super-natural dimensions. Only later, when we approach reality with more and more *a priori* filters, do we begin to see less and less of those dimensions.

G. K. Chesterton describes the simple phenomenon of an egg hatching into a baby chick. To an adult, this is a mundane thing, the simple outcome of a deterministic and uninteresting law. For a child—or a contemplative—it is magic, a miracle, creation itself. The adult greets the event with boredom, perhaps even with cynicism; the child greets it with unabashed excitement.[7]

Contemplation can restore the child's instinct for astonishment. This does not mean that the adult returns to the naive condition of a child. The critical faculty is not bypassed or denigrated by contemplative aware-ness. Rather it is stretched and opened so that what one used to see as a healthy agnosticism is now viewed as a temporary stop at a certain level of development. Con-templation brings on a "second naivete,"[8] a post-critical faculty in which, in T. S. Eliot's words:

> We shall not cease from exploration
> And the end of all our exploring
> Will be to arrive where we started
> And know the place for the first time.[9]

Since contemplation restores the early instinct for aston-ishment, it follows that it is natural to the human per-son. It is not something we must learn, but something we must relearn, and relearn again, throughout our lives.

As our range and clarity of vision progressively increases, the obscurity and impenetrability of the back-ground likewise increases. As we learn more, we also learn how much we do not know and how much there still is to learn about what we do know. To paraphrase John of the Cross, we begin to understand more by not understanding than by understanding.[10] Precisely to the degree that we begin to see things clearly, our knowledge becomes deeper, darker, and ever more ineffable.

Concomitant with all ordinary perception is a longing for unlimited being, unlimited knowing, and unlimited love. Our own personality and experience always seems too small and asphyxiating. We long to be part of everything and to have everything be part of us. This desire is realized in the union that contemplation brings about. In standing naked before reality and letting reality be for us all that it is in itself, we allow reality into our lives in such a way that it becomes part of us and we become part of it. It is through this type of union, rather than through our frenzied attempts to be everywhere at the same time through fame, travel, excessive activity, gluttonous experience, and monumental achievement, that our personalities merge with creation. The torment of the insufficiency of attainable things, the pain of our own lives never being enough for us, is overcome.

The eclipse of God is the eclipse of contemplation. The road beyond lies in a recovery of our contemplative sense.

In 1746, Denis Diderot, echoing the creed of the Enlightenment, proposed the following challenge to believers: "If the religion that you announce to me is true, its truth can be demonstrated by answerable arguments. Find these arguments. Why pursue me with prodigies, when a syllogism serves to convince me?"[11]

Centuries later, comedian Woody Allen remarks: "I am plagued by doubts. What if everything is an illusion and nothing exists? In that case I definitely overpaid for the carpet. If only God would give me some clear sign; like a large deposit in my name at a Swiss bank."[12]

God is not found at the conclusion of a syllogism, nor in a miraculous intervention in ordinary life, but in living a certain way of life. It involves every dimension of our personalities (moral, spiritual, psychological, emotional, physical, sexual, aesthetic) and every dimension of our lives (private and social). At the end of a long journey towards optimal openness, a journey that ultimately demands conversion in every dimension of our personality, God will spontaneously be part and parcel of our ordinary awareness.

Blessed are the pure in heart, for they shall see God.

Notes

1. Allan Bloom, *The Closing of the American Mind,* pp. 132–33 and 381; Philip Rieff, *The Triumph of the Therapeutic,* p. 23.

2. A theory that complements relativity that was formulated by John Bell, following Einstein, in 1965 and which has since received general acceptance in physics. The theory (of statistical correlation) indicates that at the sub-atomic level, two disparate and non-contiguous entities will, despite immense differences, manifest some very curious similarities that are rendered intelligible only if we postulate that reality is all of one piece.

3. These metaphors have a variety of sources: "eclipse of God," Martin Buber; "silence of God," I. Bergman; "living under God's shadow," F. Nietzsche; "God and religion as neurosis and guilt," S. Freud and many Neo-Freudians.

4. A brief history of the term *contemplation* is valuable in explicating its meaning: (i) In the Old Testament, there is a Hebrew word *da'ath* which connotes an intimate knowledge of something that involves your whole person. (ii) In the New Testament this concept is rendered in the Greek by the word *gnosis,* which designates an experiential knowledge, a certain intimacy (like sexual intercourse), a radical face-to-face presence of one thing to another. (iii) In the

early Greek Christian writers (e.g., Clement of Alexandria, Origen, and Gregory of Nyssa), the word *theoria* (a term borrowed from the Neoplatonists) was used to render the meaning of *gnosis*. In Neoplatonic philosophy, the term *theoria* referred to an intellectual vision of truth that the mind could contemplate ("theorize"). (iv) In the Latin writers this was rendered by the term *contemplatio*. Thus, the idea of contemplative wisdom was added to the notion of intimacy, immediacy, and experience in knowledge. This tradition was summed up by Gregory the Great in the sixth century when he described contemplation as a knowledge of God that is impregnated with love. (v) Later on in the Western mystical tradition *contemplation* came to designate something distinct from *meditation*. The distinction is drawn differently within different traditions (e.g., the Carmelite and the Ignatian) and probably dates to Hugo of St. Victor (d. 1142), who regarded *contemplatio* as the third and final stage of knowledge in the soul's ascent to unity with God; before the stage of *contemplatio* the soul must first pass through *meditatio*, a stage of preparation for unity. See Thomas Keating, *Open Mind, Open Heart* (New York: Amity Press, 1986), especially chapters 2 and 3; David Steindl-Rast, *Gratefulness the Heart of Prayer* (New York: Paulist Press, 1984), especially chapter 5, "Contemplation and Leisure"; and the article on "contemplation" in *Dictionary of Philosophy and Religion*, edited by W. L Reese (New Jersey: Humanities Press, 1980), p. 105. For a less technical account that defines the essence of contemplation magnificently, I recommend a popular book by James Finley, *The Awakening Call* (Notre Dame, Ind.: Ave Maria Press, 1984).

5. 1 Corinthians 13:12-13. The literal Greek translation reads: "For now we see as through *an enigma* (*en enigmati*)."

6. Quoted by L. Weatherhead, *The Christian Agnostic* (New York, 1965), p. 77.

7. G. K. Chesterton, *Orthodoxy* (London, 1909), pp. 90–92.

8. Paul Ricoeur is generally given credit for formulating this phrase, though my usage of it will not always and everywhere be identical with his.

9. T. S. Eliot, "Little Gidding," in *Four Quartets* (London, 1971), p. 59.

10. This is not a direct quote from John of the Cross, but captures the paradox that lies at the essence of his teaching on contemplative knowledge. The idea of "dark understanding," i.e., understanding

beyond words, concepts, and imaginative constructs, is everywhere present in his works. For more specific expressions, see *The Ascent of Mount Carmel*, book II, chapter 4, number 2; and chapters 6–12.

11. Quoted by Michael Buckley, *At the Origins of Modern Atheism*, p. 208.

12. Quoted by R. McAfee Brown, *Is Faith Obsolete* (Philadelphia, 1974), p. 86.

Part II

*Recovering the Ancient Instinct
for Astonishment: Three Contemplative
Traditions within Western Christian Thought*

four

The Purification
of Awareness

The Mystical Tradition

Waking Up

In his autobiography, *Report to Greco,* Nikos Kazantzakis tells how as a young man he went to visit a famous monk.

> Working up courage, I entered the cave and proceeded toward the voice. The ascetic was curled up on the ground. He had raised his head, and I was able in the half-light to make out his face as it gleamed in the depths of unutterable beatitude. . . .
>
> I did not know what to say, where to begin. . . . Finally I gathered up courage.
>
> "Do you still wrestle with the devil, Father Makarios?" I asked him.
>
> "Not any longer, my child. I have grown old now, and he has grown old with me. He doesn't have the strength. . . . I wrestle with God."
>
> "With God!" I exclaimed in astonishment. "And you hope to win?"

"I hope to lose, my child. My bones remain with me still, and they continue to resist."

"Yours is a hard life, Father. I too want to be saved. Is there no other way?"

"More agreeable?" asked the ascetic, smiling compassionately.

"More human, Father."

"One, only one."

"What is it?"

⸻⸻⸻ 〽 ⸻⸻⸻

God is present within us and around us,
but we are not, save for rare moments,
aware of that presence.

"Ascent. To climb a series of steps. From the full stomach to hunger, from the slaked throat to thirst, from joy to suffering. God sits at the summit of hunger, thirst, and suffering; the devil sits at the summit of a comfortable life. Choose."

"I am still young. The world is nice. I have time to choose."

Reaching out with the five bones of his hand, the ascetic touched my knee and pushed me.

"Wake up, my child. *Wake up* before death wakes you up."[1]

These words, *wake up,* concisely capture the basic prescriptive counsel of the mystical tradition of Western Christianity.

Western mysticism can also be summarized in Jesus's words: "Blessed are the pure of heart, for they shall see

God."[2] According to the great mystics, our awareness is both reduced and clouded by self-concern, excessive preoccupation with our own agendas, and with restless distractions, and we lack the purity of heart necessary to experience any God that is not of our own creation. In the mystical tradition, the road beyond practical atheism and idolatry lies in the purification of our awareness—that is, in the purging from our minds and hearts of narcissism, pragmatism, and distraction.

The tradition began to develop in the first centuries of Christianity, when the desert fathers and others took up Jesus's challenge, the pursuit of purity of heart, as the object of their monastic quest. They began to develop the idea of contemplation as a means of achieving purity, which had a strong influence on both Eastern (Greek) and the Western (Latin) Christianity. Countless men and women helped develop this tradition and mediate it down through the centuries, though its expression in the Pseudo-Dionysius around AD 500 crystallized some of its key concepts. These later influenced the great medieval, modern, and contemporary bearers of this tradition, namely, Bernard of Clairvaux, Hildegaard of Bingen, Meister Eckhardt, Jan Van Ruysbroeck, Julian of Norwich, Francis of Assisi, Thomas Aquinas, Bonaventure, John of the Cross, Teresa of Avila, Ignatius of Loyola, Greek and Russian Hesychasm, the Cloud of Unknowing, Therese of Lisieux, and Teilhard de Chardin, Catherine de Hueck Doherty, Thomas Merton, Ruth Burrows, and Henri Nouwen.

At the root of the mystical tradition is the concept that God is present within us and around us, but we are not, save for rare moments, aware of that presence.

In contemporary usage, the word *mysticism* is almost

universally misunderstood. For most people it connotes something esoteric, miraculous, and beyond, even against normal experience. Thus mystical experience is played off against ordinary experience. At its best, it is understood as the extraordinary experience of the religious elite, a high road not traveled by normal folk. At its worst, it is placed somewhere on the outer fringe where parapsychology, telepathy, and the occult meet. Rarely is it understood as connoting something to do with ordinary life.

As the tradition defines it, mysticism is, in fact, a very ordinary experience open to everyone. Mysticism describes the state of being touched by God (or anything else) in a way that is inchoate, that goes beyond what we can think, express, imagine, or clearly feel. Mystical knowledge is real knowledge, but it is "dark knowledge." We *know it,* but it is always partly ineffable, an interior knowledge that we can't conceptualize and speak about.

All of us have mystical experience, though not all of us are mystics. Mysticism is not the road of the spiritual elite or the esoteric road of the occult. It is an ordinary road for everyone. Everyone is touched in his deepest being, held, and seared by God in such a way that— unless one is hardened by sin or drugged by excessive selfishness and distraction—the presence of God is felt and progressively swells until God's reality, goodness, forgiveness, and moral demands become part of life, even if that presence cannot be articulated. If one has a pure heart, then God will color that person's heart, life, and perception, even when that presence is not explicitly self-consciousness.

The mystical presence of God depends upon purity

of heart; accordingly, the mystical tradition spells out how to rid oneself of obstacles to purity. It makes a distinction between *praxis* and *theoria*. *Praxis* is what we can do to make ourselves optimally open and receptive to the mystical presence: acts of meditation, asceticism, religious practice, moral practice, social justice, and duties of state. *Theoria* is the passive receiving of the presence of God, others, and the world. In *praxis* the heart correctly disposes itself, in *theoria* the heart receives.

The writings of the great Christian mystics are an outline what *praxis* should consist of so that purity of heart can obtained and then retained. How do we wake us, before death wakes us up?

Like a diamond that has been cut and polished over many centuries, the tradition of mysticism has too many sides to be taken in simply or seen all at once. One can only walk around it and observe it from various angles. Because of its excessive richness, I give it expression here as it is described by one of its major representatives, the Spanish mystic John of the Cross. This represents only one of its sparkles, but an important and much-venerated one. It is not better or more standard than others, but is systematic and a reliable synthesis of the tradition.

Unlike so many other mystics whose attempt to express their mystical experience does too much justice to the wildness and ineffability of that experience, John, being both an extraordinary poet and exceptional synthetic thinker, has, in a manner of speaking, been able to give left-brained expression to right-brained experience while still protecting the inchoate, dark, ineffable character of that experience. Hence, John of the Cross was chosen because, among mystics, he is exceptional in expressing somewhat the inexpressible. In his writings we find a detailed description of mysticism and clear prescriptions for attaining the purity of heart necessary to be in touch with what is mystically present within us. John presents a systematic paradigm for the purification of awareness.

The Paradigm of John of the Cross

On February 12, 1944, Anne Frank wrote these words in her diary:

> Today the sun is shining, the sky is a deep blue, there is a lovely breeze and I am longing—so longing for everything. To talk, for freedom, for friends, to be alone.
>
> And I do so long . . . to cry! I feel as if I am going to burst, and I know it would get better with crying; but I can't, I'm restless, I go from room to room, breathe through the crack of a closed window, feel my heart beating, as if it is saying, "can you satisfy my longing at last?"
>
> I believe that it is spring within me, I feel that spring is awakening, I feel it in my whole body and soul. It is an effort to behave normally. I feel utterly confused. I don't know what to read, what to write, what to do, I only know that I am longing.[3]

This kind of restlessness is what John sees as the impetus for the spiritual journey. He begins his poem "The Dark Night" with these words:

> One dark night,
> Fired with love's urgent longings. . .[4]

Just as Plato and Augustine thought before him, John believes that we are fired into life with a madness that comes from the gods and that leaves us incurably restless, seeking, longing, and insatiably drawn to a beauty, goodness, truth, and unity beyond ourselves. This restlessness is a nostalgia for the infinite, a holy eroticism, a congenital propensity to embrace everything and to become part of everything. It creates a perpetual tension at the center of our conscious and unconscious lives. We come into life neither restful nor content, but fired by love's urgent longing, our souls dis-eased in an advantageous way.

We experience these longings in many ways, both holy and unholy, during the course of our lives, and they take as their object many things. But the ultimate object of that longing is a complete and ecstatic union with God, others, and the world. We will be restless until that consummation.

This advantageous sickness constitutes the human spirit, the soul, the drive towards life. The spiritual life is the way we contain, channel, and direct the fire within us. If we use it creatively, then we are living a healthy spiritual life. If we do not, and it leads us to destructive behavior that takes us away from union God, then we are living an unhealthy spiritual life.

According to Paul in 1 Corinthians, "now we see as through a glass, darkly, but then we shall see face to face."[5] John, too, feels the union we now have is veiled, shadowy. What blocks union in our normal everyday lives?

John suggests that there are three *veils* separating us from full community with God, which must be stripped by journeying through a "dark night of the soul." This process is what the spiritual quest is all about. Our urgent longings were given to us precisely so that we might venture outward into this dark night.

The Veil of the Senses

We come into this world heavily governed by natural instinct, and our dominant instinct is for pleasure. We are naturally motivated by the desire for gratification. John calls this instinctual movement towards what gratifies us the *veil of the senses.*

When our own pleasure is the principle driving our interactions with others then we do not see others as they truly are in themselves. Imagine a baby: does it really see its mother as the mother really is? Obviously not. The baby knows and sees the mother as someone who responds to its needs. The mother's own needs, complexities, tiredness, and heartaches are not seen by the baby. The baby sees the mother in the mirror of its own need. Similarly, a sexually charged adolescent doesn't really see the girl he is looking at in all her own complexity. He sees her in the mirror of his own sexual and ego needs.

John believes there is a natural link between instinctual satisfaction and motivation to act. That is, we spontaneously operate on the pleasure principle.

The *dark night of the senses* strips this veil away. It purifies us by severing the spontaneous connection between pleasure and motivation, through an immersion into the life of Christ, and through the experience of barren.

The active part of the night of the senses is a deliberate attempt to meditate upon the life and person of
Christ and a concomitant effort to appropriate Christ's
motivation as the basis of our own action and choice. To
move beyond the attainment of pleasure and self-satis-
faction, a new motivation for action is needed. In the
active night of the senses, we study Christ's motivation
so we can imitate it in our own life.

The passive part of this dark night is the experience
and acceptance of a feeling of aridity. Like a mother
weaning a child, God dries up the feeling of satisfaction

=================== ◖ ===================

Imagine a baby: does it really see
its mother as the mother really is?

and takes away the pleasure in the things of God as well
as in things of earth. We become wearied of both God
and creature and are left with the painful feeling that
we are not serving God or our neighbor properly. We no
longer feel the enjoyment, good feelings, and security
we used to feel. John says that if we endure and persevere in prayer to God and service to others despite the
absence of all satisfaction, then we will begin to act with
a new motivation—Christ's. The connection between satisfaction and our motivation to act will have been sev-
ered. We will then act and choose not because of the
pleasure we bring ourselves but because of something
higher, namely, a desire to be of help to everything and
everybody in their struggle towards consummation and
union in love, beauty, truth, and goodness.

This change brings with it a new and purified awareness. Freed from the neediness that causes us to project
ourselves onto everything and everybody we relate to,
we can see others and the world as they are in themselves, in their own uniqueness, beauty, complexity, and
need for salvation. Once we think and feel more like
Christ, we will also *see* more like Christ. After passing
through this dark night we move beyond manipulation
to empathy, beyond clouded vision to understanding,
and beyond projection to awareness.

How do we enter into this dark night of the senses
and undergo it properly? John of the Cross gives very
clear counsels.

First, an ascetic, moral, emotional, and psychological discipline is required. What is it? One cannot enter
the dark night of the senses with any seriousness, depth,
or staying power, if there is in one's life gross moral laxity, a high level of depression, or excessive worldly distraction that will drown out deeper thoughts and voices.
As well, entry into the night depends upon regularizing
one's prayer and liturgical life.[6] Moral laxity effectively
keeps one fixed upon one's own satisfaction. Psychological and emotional depression—even physical sickness, if
too severe—tend likewise to keep us focused on ourselves
rather than on others. Constant distraction can block us
from even realizing the importance of the journey we
are invited to make.

John's first counsel can be stated as follows: Practice
moral and psychological asceticism, have a regularized
prayer life, have ecclesial involvement, don't be depres-
sively self-focused, and don't clutter up the surface of
your life with superficialities.

John then offers counsels for actively entering into

this night:[7] He tells us to meditate and study the life and person of Christ, and then to strive to imitate the motivation of Christ, by giving and receiving life in such a way that the life of the trinity can flow through you to everything and everyone you meet.

He counsels us to ascertain our motivation, and be suspicious of what fulfills our natural inclinations, be suspicious when the glory of God and our own glory habitually harmonize. We are to enter into the vulnerability of Christ, his unwillingness to protect himself against pain as he fulfills God's will.

Relativize what you think about yourself and what others think of you. We are to move beyond our need for praise, affirmation, recognition, status, and attention, and let ourself be forgotten, counted for nothing.

We are also counseled to be patient and loving enough to wait for God justify us rather than seeking self-justification. John gives this guideline:

> To reach satisfaction in all
> desire its possession in nothing.
> To come to possess all
> desire the possession of nothing.
> To arrive at being all
> desire to be nothing.
> To come to the knowledge of all
> desire the knowledge of nothing.
> To come to the pleasure you have not
> you must go by a way in which you enjoy not.
> To come to the knowledge you have not
> you must go by a way in which you know not.
> To come to the possession you have not
> you must go by a way in which you possess not.
> To come to be what you are not

you must go by a way in which you are not.
When you turn toward something
you cease to cast yourself upon the all.
For to go from all to the all
you must deny yourself of all in all.
And when you come to the possession of the all
you must possess it without wanting anything.
Because if you desire to have something in all
your treasure in God is not purely your all.[8]

John's second prescription can be summarized as follows: Make an effort to appropriate the motivation of Christ as the basis for all your actions and choices.

Lastly, John counsels us to persevere in prayer, love, and service despite the lack of gratification. Passage through the dark night of the senses demands that we accept a period, perhaps a very long one, in which we will experience virtually no pleasure or consolation in loving and serving God and others.

John's third prescription for entry into and passage through the night of the senses, then, could be put this way: Perseverance in prayer, love, and service, despite feeling no satisfaction in doing these.

The end result of this passage through the dark night of the senses will be a fundamental change in our motivation. Instead of interacting with others and the world for the gratification, satisfaction, and pleasure they bring us, we will act out of a Christ-like desire to help others in their struggle to come into a genuine community of love, beauty, truth, and goodness, and see others in the fullness of their own uniqueness, complexity, beauty, and need for salvation.

Other veils, though, still stand in the way of genuine perception and complete unity.

The Veil of the Spirit

The *dark night of the spirit* is the second phase of the purification of our awareness, and it is a far more demanding one than the first. John calls it the night of faith. Its purpose is the purification of what we rely on for knowledge, love, and security. Our heads, hearts, and persons will learn to relate, not through their normal channels of conceptual understanding, possession, and security, but through faith, charity, and hope.

John of the Cross posits that there are three major centers or "faculties of the soul" within the human person: will, intellect, and memory. It is through these interior faculties that we know and relate to that which is outside ourselves.

═══════════════ ❦ ═══════════════

John's third prescription: Perseverance in prayer,
love, and service, despite feeling no
satisfaction in doing these.

These faculties are by nature hard-wired to work spontaneously: the intellect (the head) forms concepts and images to understand and relate to reality; the will (the heart) tries to possess what it loves; and the memory (in contemporary terms, the personality or the ego) tries to control how it relates to reality and how reality relates to it so as to guarantee its own safety. Hence, we spontaneously guide our lives by conceptual knowledge, possessive love, and control designed to guarantee our own security. These faculties mediate our contact with the outside world, both making it present to us and obstructing its presence, creating yet another veil.

But, when we understand something *only* in so far as we can grasp it intellectually, and *only* in so far as we can possess it, and *only* in so far as we can remain in control and secure in the face of it, we relate only partially to that reality. Imagine a good photograph of your mother—perhaps it captures her character in an exceptional way. That is all well and good, but it is still not your mother! Her reality is infinitely larger, richer, and more complex than what that photograph or a million others can capture. Our conceptual understanding functions similarly. Through the concepts and the imaginative pictures that our heads spontaneously construct, we see each other and the world outside ourselves as we see our mother in a photograph—it is her, but her actual reality dwarfs the photograph. The natural bent of the heart to possess and the personality to find security limit us in the same way. Good as these natural inclinations are, they ultimately block true perception and true relationship.

The dark night of the spirit can open our heads, hearts, and personalities to a new way of understanding, loving, and relating. Without destroying or denigrating their natural functions, this transformation stretches the natural capacities of these three faculties to their optimum state.

The intellect moves beyond its natural reliance on concepts and images to understand and know to a new type of knowledge—*faith;* the will moves beyond possessive love to a new type of love—*charity;* and the personality (ego) moves beyond security to a new type of reassurance—*hope.* With this transformation we are open to a whole new awareness, a mystical awareness. But because our heads, hearts, and egos are no longer linked in their normal way to what is outside them, this new awareness is initially quite painful and is felt as a kind of darkness.

What causes the head to move from a reliance on concepts to a reliance on faith? Or the will to move from a reliance on possession to a reliance on charity? Or the personality to move from a reliance on security and control to trusting in hope?

We enter into the dark night of the spirit when we make the decision to live by raw faith.

The active aspect begins when a person makes the choice to guide his life on the basis of God's word alone like Abraham, who "set out without knowing where he was going."[9] If we try to understand through faith, love through charity, and relate through hope, God does the rest.

We will begin to feel the withering of all the understanding, support, and consolation that we used to derive from the intellectual concepts, possessive love, and the control we exercised in our lives. John tells us this will lead to great desolation. No longer able to derive any support from our natural faculties, we experience a horrible emptiness, a sense of weakness, a feeling of abandonment . . . "the soul feels that God has rejected it and with an abhorrence of it casts it into darkness."[10] Still, deprived of their normal way of relating to the world, our intellect, will and memory begin to rely on faith, hope, and charity.

Our perception is purified in a surprising number of ways. First, we no longer see things through the medium of the intellect's imaginative pictures. Rather, we look at them in their totality and wildness. Instead of seeing things in terms of possessive love, we now see them in all their richness, complexity, and beauty. The possessive gaze of lust and jealousy turns into the look of admiration. Instead of allowing the reality of the other into our life only insofar as we can control it, we now see and grasp reality in its fullness, complete with aspects that threaten our security. That kind of relating is what constitutes faith, hope, and charity.

John gives very clear counsel on how one is to enter this night and remain in it. The *praxis* required to enter the night of the spirit is reliance upon faith alone. A person must take the articles of faith and use them to make his decisions, choices, and actions: "Like a blind man he must lean on dark faith, accept it for his guide and light, and rest on nothing of what he understands, tastes, feels, or imagines. All these perceptions are a darkness that will lead him astray. Faith lies beyond all this understanding, tasting, feeling, and imagining. If he does not blind himself in these things and abide in total darkness, he will not reach what is greater—the teaching of faith."[11]

John's counsel: Let the articles of faith, not your feelings and knowledge and need for security, become your guide for living! You will then look at everything and everyone with the eyes of Christ. One veil remains to be stripped away.

The Veil of Life

Part of what blocks us from seeing face-to-face is natural life itself. Human nature, of itself, is an impediment to full consummation with God, others and the world.

Once the veil of the senses and of the spirit have been lifted, one is aware "that nothing is wanting other than to tear the weak veil of this natural life, in which it feels the entanglement, hindrance, and captivity of its freedom, and since it desires to be dissolved and to be with Christ, it laments that a life so weak and base impedes another so mighty and sublime."[12]

---

*Let the articles of faith, not your feelings
and knowledge and need for security, become
your guide for living! You will then look at
everything and everyone with the eyes of Christ.*

It is possible to explain this concept too simplistically in terms of classical dualism, which sees the body as something to be escaped from so that full union can take place in heaven. John is a dualist, but he does not mean the limitations he is speaking about—the final bondage that must be stripped away by death—to be understood in the sense that the soul is pure and can fly but the body is sinful and weighs one down, making salvation largely an escape from flesh. No. For John, our human nature simply limits us while we are in this world: we can only be at one place at one time; our capacity for love is limited, we cannot be polymorphously loving and sexual, but must choose between monogamy and promiscuity; our capacity for understanding is limited too, not only because we see from a limited perspective, but because we must conceptualize and speak within the framework of a very finite system of symbols; and the human heart and personality, tied to natural instinct and human nature, can never move to the fullness of perception and love. We are, in this life, too incurably human!

Death brings about the final purification, not by making us a-cosmic—angels who no longer have bodies, but by making us pan-cosmic—spirits with the entire cosmos for a body.

John of the Cross's three dark nights are really one transformative journey that leads by way of a series of reversals, disappointments, sacrifice, and suffering to a radically purified awareness. With this comes a disclosure of God. God is now known through mystical union, in dark knowledge, through "understanding by not understanding" than through a more intellectual understanding. This is knowledge in the biblical sense, in which one does not intellectually grasp God, or, at the level of feeling, does not have the awareness and security that God is real. Rather there is an inchoate sense that our every breath and our every second is held in existence and guided by a God who cannot be grasped but who can be touched and felt in love.

The Mystical Purification of Natural Wonder

When John of the Cross described the dark night, he was writing for persons who were already far advanced in the spiritual journey and for whom the radical question of God's existence was not an issue. He did not envisage the self-preoccupied crowd in the marketplace whom Nietzsche's madman accuses of killing God. But his paradigm is not just for the advanced phases of people's

prayer lives; it is true for purification of human perception and awareness in general. Ultimately, he is describing the intrinsic link between morality and
epistemology, that is, how the accuracy and fullness of
perception depends upon the faith, charity, and hope of
the perceiver. Contemplative wonder, proper perception, passes through identical stages (as Christian
prayer) and depends upon the same conditions for its
purification.

John's paradigm can help us decondition ourselves
from the distortions of perception and so regain our
contemplative faculties. The dark night of the soul can
help us restore our sense of wonder by giving us the
asceticism we need to move beyond the spontaneous dictates of our own narcissism; by breaking our self-centeredness and pragmatism as the motivation for our
knowing and loving; and by moving us beyond the
propensity to relate through conceptual understanding,
possessive feelings, and the need for security.

To understand how the dark night of the soul accom-
plishes this triple purification within us, we must first
examine how we are triply blocked.

Firstly, lack of moral, emotional, and psychological
discipline reduces wonder because it invariably leads to
self-indulgence and self-preoccupation—the antitheses
of genuine awareness. When you are preoccupied with
the self, the other is seen not as it is in itself, but only as
it is in relation to you.

Examples abound. Anyone who does not check his
feelings of paranoia, self-pity, and resentment quite vig-
orously at times will invariably find himself caught up in
a depressive self-focus that has a double effect: since
depression focuses us upon ourselves, it further limits

what we notice and are aware of; it also distorts what we perceive with paranoia and suspicion. Moral laxity similarly limits and distorts awareness. The person who is sexually indulgent will invariably see others, not as they are in themselves, but as sex objects, as sexual rivals, or as uninteresting because they are not sexually attractive.

Secondly, our pragmatic and narcissistic concerns narrow awareness accordingly. Reality is not perceived as it is in itself, with all its multifarious dimensions and its riches; it is only seen as it relates to our needs and concerns.

Imagine entering a crowded train station in search of a friend. As you scan the crowd of faces your eyes see hundreds of faces, but your awareness of these others is superficial and virtually non-existent. You are looking for a particular face and you focus on nothing else. Your pragmatic concern, valid in itself, dictates that you are open to only one face, your friend's. Whenever reality is approached pragmatically, we will notice only certain of its dimensions, although, as this illustration makes clear, there are many other dimensions present to perceive.

Thirdly, every imaginative construct for understanding and every feeling through which we possess something is ultimately inadequate. In the end, these are icons that conceal as much as they reveal. When in response to our natural instincts we seek to understand in a conceptual way, when we seek to control our relationship to people and things in order to feel secure, then we never fully attain the sheer gaze of admiration, the full gift of wonder.

Imagine someone telling you: "I understand you. I've watched you grow up, I know your Myers-Briggs results,

I know your Enneagram number, and I am familiar with the dysfunctions in your family background. Besides that, you are French, and I know the temperament of the French! And you are so perfectly your mother's daughter! Oh, yes, I understand you!" Would you feel very understood? No. I think you would not. You would feel reduced. But someone who says: "You know, I don't understand you at all! You are one rich mystery! I've known you for twenty years and you still constantly surprise me!" I suspect that you would make you feel more understood and whole.

The dark night of the spirit that John of the Cross prescribes for the purification of our prayer lives is equally necessary for the purification of our awareness. Unless our normal way of understanding is transformed we will never truly stand before each other and the world in wonder.

Nikos Kazantzakis once said:

Truly, nothing more resembles God's eyes than the eyes of a child; they see the world for the first time, and create it. Before this, the world is chaos. All creatures—animals, trees, men, stones, everything: forms, colors, voices, smells, lightning flashes—flow unexplored in front of the child's eyes (no, not in front of them, inside them), and he cannot fasten them down, cannot establish order. The child's world is not made of clay, to last, but of clouds. A cool breeze blows across his temples and the world condenses, attenuates, vanishes. Chaos must have passed in front of God's eyes in just this way before the Creation. . . .[13]

Kazantzakis adds: "When I was a child, I became one with sky, insects, sea, wind—whatever I saw or touched. . . . Shutting my eyes contentedly, I used to hold out my palms and wait. God always came—as long as I remained a child."[14] The mystical tradition within Christianity assures us of the same thing. God will always come to us . . . as long as we, through the painful purification of our awareness that they describe, remain in the perceptive posture of a child.

Notes

1. Nikos Kazantzakis, *Report to Greco* (New York, 1965), pp. 222–23.

2. Matthew 5:8.

3. Anne Frank, *The Diary of a Young Girl* (New York: Doubleday, 1967), p. 134.

4. John of the Cross, *The Dark Night of the Soul,* book II, chapter 19, no. 1, Kavanaugh, *op. cit.,* p. 373.

5. 1 Corinthians 13:12–13 (my translation).

6. For example: *The Dark Night of the Soul,* book I, chapter 9, clearly spells out that one will not pass through the *night of the senses* if there is habitual moral laxity ("sin and imperfection"), no regular life of prayer ("weakness and lukewarmness"), and too severe a level of psychological depression ("bad humor or bodily indisposition"). The "drowning out of God's voice by constant distraction" is clearly outlined, among other places, in *The Living Flame of Love,* commentary on stanza 3, nos. 18–23.

7. John of the Cross, *The Ascent of Mount Carmel,* book I, chapter 13, Kavanaugh, pp. 101–4.

8. John of the Cross, *The Ascent of Mount Carmel,* book I, chapter 13, no. 11, Kavanaugh, pp. 103–4.

9. Hebrews 11:8.

10. John of the Cross, *The Ascent of Mount Carmel,* book II, chapter 6, Kavanaugh, pp. 119–21. For a detailed description of the pains, emptiness, and afflictions experienced in the passive night of the

spirit, see *The Dark Night of the Soul,* book II, chapters 5–8, Kavanaugh, pp. 335–46.

11. John of the Cross, *The Ascent of Mount Carmel,* book II, chapter 4, Kavanaugh, pp. 112–15.

12. John of the Cross, *The Living Flame of Love,* commentary on stanza one, nos. 29–32, Kavanaugh, pp. 591–92.

13. Nikos Kazantzakis, *Report to Greco,* pp. 44–45. In Christian spirituality there is an interesting connection between seeing and sanctity (a connection not as pronounced in other traditions, even other mystical traditions). In Christianity, the eyes are very important. G. K. Chesterton contrasts how Christian saints are depicted in art with how Buddhist saints are depicted: "The opposition exists at every point; but perhaps the shortest statement of it is that the Buddhist saint always has his eyes shut, while the Christian saint always has them wide open. The Buddhist saint has a sleek and harmonious body, but his eyes are heavy and sealed with sleep. The medieval saint's body is wasted to its crazy bones, but his eyes are frightfully alive. . . . The Buddhist is looking with a peculiar intentness inward. The Christian is staring with frantic intentness outward" (G. K. Chesterton, *Everlasting Man* [New York, 1955], p. 241).

14. Nikos Kazantzakis, *Report to Greco,* p. 45.

five

Contemplation as Respecting the Holiness of God

The Protestant Contemplative Tradition

In her book *Holy the Firm*, Annie Dillard shares with us her quandary about deciding which church to attend:

> Nothing could more surely convince me of God's unending mercy than the continued existence on earth of the church.
>
> The higher Christian churches—where, if any-where, I belong—come at God with an unwar-ranted air of professionalism, with authority and pomp, as though they knew what they were doing, as though people in themselves were an appropriate set of creatures to have dealings with God. I often think of the set pieces of liturgy as certain words which people have successfully addressed to God with their getting killed. In the high churches they saunter through liturgy like Mohawks along a strand of scaffolding who have long since forgotten their danger. If God were to blast such a service to bits, the congregation would be, I believe, genuinely shocked. But in the

low churches you expect it any minute. This is the beginning of wisdom.[1]

It is also, in a large segment of Christian thought, the beginning of contemplation.

In the tradition of classical Protestantism, contemplation is understood as a healthy fear of the Lord, in which we let God be God and live in the face of that holiness. It is the essence of what classical Protestantism considers "purity of heart"—living by faith rather than by understanding, living in humility rather than in boasting, letting God give us justification rather than attempting to grasp it ourselves.

Isaiah's reminder that "God's ways are not our ways,"[2] God's reminder to Job that anyone who was not around when the foundations of the universe were being laid should be more filled with wonder and less with conclusions,[3] and Paul's reminder that we can approach God only through faith and that we depend for life upon his justification rather than upon our own[4] contain the seeds of Protestantism contemplation. Living those truths is contemplation.

Classical Protestantism embodies this tradition, and the very word *Protestant* implies it. The protest of Luther and the original reformers was not, as is commonly supposed, a protest against Rome and the Roman church. It was first and foremost a protest for God, a protest against every private and institutional thought or practice that in any way denigrated the absolute holiness and freedom of God, or that attempted to approach God through the categories of human reason rather than those of faith. It is clearly represented in the thought of Luther and Calvin. More recently it is less clearly manifest along denominational lines, and so can be seen in Protestant, Anglican, and Roman Catholic circles alike. In Protestantism today it is seen in the thought of Karl Barth and his Neo-Orthodox followers and, with a slightly different nuance, in Jürgen Moltmann. Among Roman Catholic and Anglican/Episcopalian thinkers it is manifest in the writings of Hans Urs Von Balthasar, Gustavo Gutiérrez, and Alan Jones.

Among all these thinkers, past and present, is the idea that the experience of the death of God is due to a breakdown in contemplation, and, for them, to contemplate is to live always in a holy fear of God.

The Loss of the Sense of God's Holiness

G. K. Chesterton once commented that our perennial spiritual and psychological task is *to* learn to look at things familiar until they become unfamiliar again.[5] The Protestant contemplative tradition would agree and insist that this is nowhere more imperative than in our relationship with God, the Holy One.

God, as scripture and church teachings assure us, is holy. Holiness, however, must be properly understood. It does not mean piety, as we commonly assume. Biblically, holiness means otherness, incomprehensibility, beyond conception, beyond imagination, awesome, awe-ful. As the holy, God is antithetical to finite creatures. The infinite is not like the finite.[6] When Isaiah has his vision of God in the temple and is left gasping and simply repeating the words "Holy, Holy, Holy is the Lord

God of hosts,"[7] his words might be paraphrased: "Other, awesome, completely beyond what I can see, think, feel, imagine, or capture in words is the Lord God of hosts!" Isaiah then goes on to say that our response to this holiness must be a holy fear, an acceptance of the fact that in our understanding we can never capture God or understand his ways.

The concept of God's otherness and our need to respect it is central to the teachings of the New Testament. Not only is it the pivotal theme of Paul's letters (especially to the Romans and Galatians) but Jesus makes a pedagogy of it in his revelation of God. The parables, for example, are iconoclastic, subverting and smashing people's familiar notions of God in such a way that out of the ruins comes an invitation to a new understanding of God. In Jesus's entire revelation, but especially in the parables, there is the challenge to let God be God.

Although the stories in Jesus's parables are about people, the real plot is God. They are revelatory, revealing the heart of God. They teach us that the divine mystery cannot be pinned down or figured out by human projections and expectations. It is dangerous to suppose that God must feel and think as we do! The parables try to move us beyond that temptation. They show us a God whose heart is full of surprises and who has perspectives far beyond ours. This is depicted with unequivocal clarity in the parable of the prodigal son[8]—none of Christ's listeners could have anticipated the Father's reaction, in the parable of the vineyard workers[9]—who would have surmised that the last workers would receive the same pay as the first ones?, and in the parable of the good Samaritan[10]—who would have foretold that the priest would pass by and the enemy, the Samaritan, would stop?

There is always an element of surprise in the parables, and in Christ's revelation in general. The logic and measured expectations of those hearing revelation is always shattered. Jesus's listeners would felt this astonishment. In John Shea's words, God was always *more* than they had anticipated:

For as Mark says,

> "He was too much for them."
> Like a woman who loves too much
> like ointment that costs too much
> and is spilled too much
> like a seventy times seven God
> who forgives too much
> like a seed that grows too much
> and yields thirty
> > sixty
> > a hundred fold.[11]

Christ is telling us: "Do not try to capture God. Live in wonder. Let your agnosticism be very very wide. Do not try to understand the infinite within the confines of finite experience."

Invariably, however, that is precisely what we try to do by approaching God through the categories of human understanding rather than through the categories of faith, making God meet human expectations, metaphysical, psychological, or moral. We also do it by attempting to be our own justification rather then letting God give us righteousness. The purity of heart needed for contemplation breaks down and God eventually dies in our experience.

Job's Friends

The Protestant contemplative tradition understands that the God of Judeo-Christian and Islamic revelation (as well as the God of Hinduism, Buddhism, and Taoism) is infinite and, therefore, ungraspable by the finite human mind or heart. Such a God is, by definition, not able to be conceptualized or imagined. So, too, are the ways of that God. A proper relationship to God can only be one of backing off and giving God the space in which to be God. Unlike Job's friends, we must avoid the idea that God thinks, feels, acts, and is as we are. However subtle it might be, not to do so is to make God less than God and to fall out of contemplation.

─────────── ◊ ───────────

There is always an element of surprise in the parables, and in Christ's revelation in general.

─────────────────────────

Several years ago, Harold Kushner published *When Bad Things Happen to Good People*,[12] which immediately became a best-seller. It is a deeply compassionate reflection on human suffering and how God might be conceived of in the light of our suffering. Kushner asks how can God be all-loving and all-powerful in light of the fact that there is so much random and senseless suffering on earth? Young children die of cancer. Young mothers whose children desperately need them are struck down through accidents and illness. There is so much inexplicable suffering. How can God permit this?

Kushner's question is not new; it is the perennial question about suffering and evil. What is novel, within both the tradition of Judaism (from which he comes) and Christianity, is his answer. God is all-loving. But our unredeemed suffering shows us that God is not all-powerful. Kushner says that if God had the radical power to stop random suffering he would; since he does not, we can conclude that he does not have the power to.

Kushner is more in line with Job's friends than with Job. Despite his deep compassion, his thesis is, ultimately, an example, and a very good one at that, of psychological univocity. He says that since *we* cannot make sense of something then *that something cannot make sense at all.* There is no perspective beyond our own. There is no higher perspective from which what we cannot understand might be understood. Whatever else this conception is, in the end, it is a slimming down of God to fit the size, expectations, and reasoning of the human mind and imagination. The infinite is being understood by way of the finite. Perhaps this serves to make God more accessible to us and allows us to understand God's compassion more easily. But it has, according to the Protestant tradition of contemplation, a potentially lethal dysfunction: a God who is not allowed to be God beyond our human understanding and imagination will in due time be rejected for being less than God!

Several years ago, Gordon Sinclair, a famous Canadian journalist, died. For many years he had been a regular panelist on a nationally televised news program. An avowed atheist, Sinclair had for years given the

Canadian public his apologia for atheism. As a young journalist he had gone to India to cover the wars surrounding India's struggles with Britain and saw human misery and death of such a magnitude that his mind and heart simply could not reconcile with the existence of God. In Sinclair's words, "God is simply not imaginable in the face of that kind of suffering and meaninglessness."

Had he presented this apologia to Isaiah, Job, Luther, or Calvin he would have received a surprising answer. They would have said: "You're right! In the face of that kind of suffering, one cannot *imagine* that God exists! But belief in God and faith in God is not had on the basis of being able to *imagine* his existence. In fact, if you try to imagine God, and look very hard at certain issues, you will end up an atheist!" Why? Because all attempts to picture God and to understand rationally how the existence of such a Being can be consistent with what we see in life is an enterprise that, by definition, undercuts our ability to believe in God.

Looking at the perennial presence of suffering and evil in the world, one could argue, as many do, that God either cannot exist, exists but is not all-powerful, or is malicious and incompetent. Our world is too full of physical and moral evil—infectious parasites, cancer, AIDS, and natural disasters that inflict death, pain, and destruction; and cruelty (even among children), selfishness, exploitation, rape, murder, insensitivity and stupidity.[13] With evil so widespread, how can we conceive of a benevolent, all-powerful creator who is lovingly coaxing creation to higher levels of existence?

Perhaps even more challenging is the task of trying

to conceive of the existence of God in the face of the overwhelming immensity of the universe and the infinite multiplicity of phenomena within it. When one goes out at night and looks at the stars, the light of those closest to us, travelling at the unimaginable speed of 186,000 miles per second, has taken four years to reach our eyes. The light from those that are most distant from us has taken 800,000 years to reach us . . . and scientists have seen stars through x-ray telescopes whose light has not yet reached the earth, stars that are six trillion light years from our earth. The enormity of our universe stuns the imagination. These distances cannot be conceived of. Given that there are perhaps hundreds of billions of galaxies with trillions of light years separating them, and given that on each of the planets within each of those galaxies there are hundreds of trillions of phenomena occurring every second over billions of years, can we really believe that somewhere there is a person, a heart so supreme that it created all this? And that, right now, it knows minutely and intimately every detail and that it is passionately concerned with every event?

Our planet is one of many billions of planets. During each second of time on earth thousands of people are being born, thousands are being conceived, thousands of others are dying, are sinning, are doing virtuous acts, are suffering, celebrating, hoping, praying, despairing, and all of this has been happening for hundreds of thousands of years. Can we really believe that a God exists who is Lord over all of this so that "no sparrow falls from the sky or no hair from a human head" without that Lord knowing and caring deeply?

The answer is *no!* When one considers evil and the

sheer immensity of phenomena, one cannot conceive of a God who could truly be lord and master of it all. Our minds and imaginations cannot stretch far enough. We cannot *picture* it. But that is precisely the point: the divine reality cannot be grasped through a finite imagination. The limits of human imagination and its frustrations vis-à-vis imagining the existence of God are not the same as the existence or non-existence of God. The fact that we cannot imagine God speaks more about the finitude of the mind than it does about the likelihood or unlikelihood of the existence of an infinite being.

Many difficulties arise from our failure to recognize and appropriate this. Suppose one night I lie in bed and stare holes in the darkness, trying to imagine the existence of God. But I cannot and I begin to panic: "Dear God, I am an atheist! I can no longer imagine and feel that God exists! God doesn't exist!" On another night, I lie in bed and I feel very secure in my sense that God exists and I can imagine that existence. Does this mean that on the one night I have no faith in God and on the other I do have faith? It would be more accurate to say that one night I have a weak imagination and on the other night I have a strong one! The difference lies not in God's existence or non-existence, but in the capacity or incapacity of the imagination to crank up its own constructs which either give one the sense that God exists or leave one unable to feel it.

Frustrations in attempting to conceive of and feel God's relationship to creation tend to lead, as they did in Gordon Sinclair's case, to the unfounded conclusion that, because we cannot think, picture, or understand how it is possible, then God does not exist. The atheism that arises from our incapacity to conceive of God is an idolatry that results from not properly respecting God's holiness. A God that has been slimmed down to fit the limits of a finite heart and mind is unable to measure up intellectually because (and this is a strange paradox) an intellectually conceivable God is, ultimately, inconceivable intellectually.

Where does that leave us? If God cannot be conceived of, how can we know God? Are we doomed to either agnosticism or blind faith based solely on authority and revelation?

For the Protestant contemplative tradition there is another option: awe and wonder! God cannot be *thought,* but God can be *met.* He can be experienced, touched, and encountered. In such a posture to God, we live in contemplation.

Human Boasting

To let God be God means not only that we do not set limits to the infinite, but also that we allow God to give us meaning, significance, uniqueness, and eternal life. To be a contemplative means that we must not "boast" but must be "saved by faith alone."[14]

Alan Jones, who straddles a number of contemplative traditions, including this one, succinctly states:

> We nurse within our hearts the hope that we are different, that we are special, that we are extraordinary. We long for the assurance that our birth was no accident, that a god had a hand in our coming to be, that we exist by divine fiat. We

ache for a cure for the ultimate disease of mortality. Our madness comes when the pressure is too great and we fabricate a vital lie to cover up the fact that we are mediocre, accidental, mortal. We fail to see the glory of the Good News. The vital lie is unnecessary because all the things we long for have been given us freely.[15]

One of our great temptations in life is this vital lie, what scripture calls "boasting" and "self-righteousness." As Jones points out, we are born with the innate knowledge, we are wired to the fact that we are unique, significant, precious, and destined for eternal life. But this intuition, however deeply felt, tends to wilt under the pressure of trying to live a life that is unique and special in a world in which billions of others are trying to do the same thing. Can billions be infinitely precious and utterly unique?

Inevitably the fear of anonymity and mortality overwhelms us. When we feel this—and outside of a deep faith it can be the dominant feeling during the second half of our lives—we begin to believe that we are meaningful *only* when we accomplish something that sets us apart and ensures that we will be remembered. For most of us, the dominant obsession of adult life is trying to guarantee our own preciousness, lovableness, meaning, immortality, and sanctity. We do not believe we can have these independent of our own accomplishments. And so we fabricate the lie, we try to make a mark for ourselves.

In the tradition of Protestantism, contemplation means that we do not attempt to be justified by anything or anybody other than God alone. *Faith alone saves!* That simple line contains the Protestant counsel for contemplation: Let God give you preciousness, meaning, significance, and eternal life. Do not try to guarantee these for yourself. To let God be holy, and to let God's ways be above our ways, means that we must trust God to give us these things *beyond* our ways.

Contemplation as Faith

Jürgen Moltmann captures the essence of the Protestant contemplative tradition in the following quote:

> The cross is the utterly incommensurable factor in the revelation of God. We have become far too used to it. We have surrounded the scandal of the cross with roses. We have made a theory of salvation out of it. But that is not the cross. That is not the blackness inherent in it, placed in it by God. Hegel defined the cross: "God is dead"—and he no doubt rightly saw that here we are faced with the night of the real, ultimate and inexplicable absence of God, and that before the "Word of the cross" we are dependent upon the principle *sola fide;* dependent upon it as nowhere else. Here we have not the *opera dei,* which point to him as the eternal creator, and to his wisdom. Here the faith in creation, the source of all paganism, breaks down. Here this whole philosophy and wisdom is abandoned to folly. Here God is non-God. Here is the triumph of death, the enemy, the non-church, the lawless state, the blasphemer, the soldiers. Here Satan triumphs over God. *Our faith begins at the point where atheists suppose that it must be at an end. Our faith*

begins with the bleakness and power which is the night of the cross, abandonment, temptation, and doubt about everything that exists!

Our faith must be born where it is abandoned by all tangible reality; it must be born of nothingness, it must taste this nothingness and be given it to taste in a way no philosophy of nihilism can imagine.[16]

═══════════════ ❦ ═══════════════

Let God give you preciousness, meaning, significance, and eternal life. Do not try to guarantee these for yourself.

═══════════════════════════════════

Contemplation means living in such a way that God can enter into our lives. There are many ways of being open to God. *Metaphysically* it means that the difference between God and creature is infinitely greater than any similarity, as the Fourth Lateran Council (1215) taught.[17] Consequently the Protestant tradition would not conclude that bad things happening to good people implies that God is not all-powerful. The metaphysical and religious speculations of Job's friends block true contemplation.

Psychologically and intellectually it means that we must respect the fact that all concepts we form of God and God's ways are fundamentally inadequate to understand God.

Emotionally it means that we must learn to live with the insecurity of an understanding of God that is not intellect based, and must accept mystery, unsolved riddles, and unrequited emotional suffering.

Contemplation means living in what mystics have always described as a certain emotional and intellectual darkness. God can reveal himself to us only when we do not block that revelation with our heads, our emotions, and our actions.

As Moses approached the burning bush, God told him: "Take off your shoes because the ground you are standing on is holy ground!"[18] Elizabeth Barrett Browning paraphrased God's invitation to Moses and offered a universal prescription for contemplation: "The earth is ablaze with the fire of God, but only those who see it take their shoes off. The rest sit around and pick blackberries!"[19] The crowd in Nietzsche's marketplace have been caught with their shoes on, picking blackberries!

How do we translate these concepts into a contemplative *praxis?* In the practical task of living, how do we let God be God?

Four prescriptive counsels outline contemplation in the Protestant tradition. We are to approach God through faith, not understanding; undergo God's presence rather than trying to understand it; live in holy fear of God; and let justify you rather than trying to guarantee your own justification.

Faith, Not Understanding

Understanding takes place on the basis of intellectual and imaginative constructs. Faith takes place on the basis of trust. Our natural inclination is to demand understanding and to feel uncomfortable and impatient without it. This proclivity to make sense of everything rather than to live in a more far-reaching trust is a God-given instinct and is both good and necessary for us to live as human beings. It serves us well in most realms. But it does not serve us well in terms of our relationship to God. As we saw with the mystical tradition, it must ultimately be transcended to live in faith.

The difference between understanding and faith becomes clearer when we look at some examples. Henri Nouwen offers a gripping one from his own life.

In *In Memoriam,* he describes the death of his mother, beginning with his feelings as he flies home from New York to Amsterdam to be at her side. His mother had been a wonderful, generous, very Christian, very loving woman, and Nouwen expected that her death would radiate those qualities. He thinks of her in gratitude and imagines that her death will be a capstone on a gracious and Christian life.

The reality that confronts him at her bedside shatters his naive expectations. His mother lies dying, not in the calm of peace, but in the grip of struggle, even terror.

> Why, why were we witnessing such pain and agony in a woman whose life had been one of goodness, gentleness, tenderness and love . . . ?
>
> During the days of mother's dying, I heard that question repeated frequently. Often, friends suggested that it was unfair for this lovely woman to suffer such a painful death. Many were adamant that she did not deserve such a wrenching struggle. But do we really understand?
>
> Slowly, as the long hours and days passed, I

began to wonder if mother's struggle did not in fact reveal the awesome truth of God's love. Who was more loving than Jesus? Who suffered more than he? Jesus's life of faithful service did not end in a peaceful, tranquil death. He who was without sin suffered an agony of immeasurable depth; his cry of the cross, "God, O God, why have you forsaken me?" still echoes down through the centuries.

Is it this agony that mother was called to share? Is it this cross that she was invited to feel more deeply than others? I do not know. I cannot say yes or no to these questions. What really took place during the hours of her death cannot be explained or made understandable. But the thought that she who had loved so many, given so much and felt so deeply, was called to be united with Christ even in his agony, did not leave me during these days.

Friends kept saying to me, "Your mother always thought of others first": That is true. She lived for others, for her husband, her children, her grandchildren, her friends. She indeed had the mind of Christ, always considering the other person to be better than her self. But that does not necessarily lead to a smooth death. Why do we think that the hope for a life with Christ will make our death like a gentle passage? A compassionate life is a life in which the suffering of others is deeply felt, and such a life may also make one's death an act of dying with others. When I saw mother's battle, her cry of hope and faith, I wondered if she was not crying with the many others for whom she had lived.

In Jesus's agony we see the agony of the world in all its gripping intensity: Sadness came over him, and great distress. Then he said . . . "My soul is sorrowful to the point of death" (Matthew 26:37). Is not every human being who wants to live with the mind of Christ also called to die with the mind of Christ? . . .

What then is this agony? Is it fear of God, fear of punishment, fear of the immensity of the divine presence? I do not know, but if I have any sense of what I saw, it was more profound. It was the fear of the great abyss which separates God from us, a distance which can only be bridged by faith.[20]

Nouwen describes the movement from understanding to faith, from a reliance upon knowledge to trust. When the wells of logical expectations, feeling, imagination, and intellectual understanding run dry, when obfuscation threatens to turn to despair, when it seems impossible to feel God's existence and goodness in the face of some concrete fact, the contemplative continues to live in an openness to God.

In affirming that faith is not understanding, this tradition does not affirm that faith *goes against* understanding or that faith is based upon blind trust. Faith takes us *beyond* understanding, but does not denigrate it any more than Einstein's physics denigrates grade-school arithmetic, or reality denigrates a photograph, or the light of dawn denigrates a candle burning in the night. It just goes infinitely beyond it. What was grasped in the mind and heart before faith's light eclipsed it was real and remains so. The trust in which we now live takes its root in there. Grade-school arithmetic is still valid after Einstein, a photograph is still real even when you actually see the person in it, and a candle still gives off light even when a bright sun eclipses it; they remain as the foundation from which we move on to a trust in what is greater than they are.

Undergo God's Presence

Within the Protestant contemplative tradition the presence of God is not something to be studied, analyzed, conceptualized, figured out, or captured. As John Shea so aptly put it: "God is not a law to be obeyed but a presence to be seized and acted on."[21]

In an analogy that comes from Jesus—"Take the fig tree as a parable; as soon as its twigs grow supple and its leaves come out, you know that summer is near"[22]—letting God be God means undergoing the presence of God as a tree undergoes the presence of summer. The metaphor is simple and perfectly apt: a tree is brought to bloom by summer. It does not understand summer, conceptualize summer, nor is it able to project what summer will do to it; it simply acts under its presence. To let God be God is to live in openness to the mystery of God without limiting the nature or effect of his presence by any expectations or by withdrawal. The task of contemplation is not to specify what conditions must be met before we believe in God's existence, power, or goodness. Rather the task of contemplation is to let God be God, and like the fig tree, act under his presence. The proper approach to God is not to try to analyze the infinite, but to celebrate it.

Then, in the face of all the hard agnostic and bitter questions concerning evil, suffering, and God's apparent absence and impotence, we will be drawn into the posture of the mature Job. When he finally let God be God, he exclaimed:

Faith takes us beyond understanding, but does not denigrate it any more than Einstein's physics denigrates grade-school arithmetic, or reality denigrates a photograph, or the light of dawn denigrates a candle burning in the night.

I know that you are all-powerful;
what you conceive, you can perform.
I am the man who has obscured your designs
with my empty-headed words.
I have been holding forth on matters I cannot
    understand,
on marvels beyond me and my knowledge . . .
My words have been frivolous: What can I reply?
I had better lay my finger on my lips.
I have spoken once . . . I will not speak again;
More than once . . . I will add nothing.[23]

Live in Holy Fear of God

Fear of the Lord is the beginning of wisdom. This kind of fear has none of the pejorative connotations this expression brings to mind, namely, fear that God will punish us if we do not do good; that we should submit to God out of timidity or cowardice; that our own achievements somehow threaten God; or fear of truly enjoying our lives we feel that somehow we are stealing pleasure from God. All of these are unhealthy fears are psychologically rooted, and are antithetical to a truly holy fear of God.

G. K. Chesterton once suggested that "the greatest of all illusions is the illusion of familiarity."[24] Familiarity is also the death of respect, wonder, and awe. When our minds, hearts, and imaginations are no longer poised for surprise and astonishment, then we no longer have a healthy fear of God or indeed of each other, which means living in such a way that nothing becomes too familiar to us.

We can understand this more clearly if we look at where holy fear breaks down in our interpersonal relations. When we examine our deepest resentments, we invariably find that at their roots lies the fact that someone has not respected us. Usually the violation is not blatant. Almost always it is subtle: someone has taken us for granted, has assumed that he understands us and our motives, has boxed us in with her own preconceived notions of who we are; has not respected our uniqueness, mystery, and complexity; or has taken as owed to them what we can only offer as gift. This is a picture of the illusion of familiarity, and it is what is expressed in the axiom "familiarity breeds contempt."

By extension, to live in fear of God means that we

live before God and the rest of reality in such a way that there is never contempt within us. We take nothing for granted, everything as a gift. We have respect. We are always poised for surprise before the mystery of God, others, and ourselves. All boredom and contempt is an infallible sign that we have fallen out of a healthy fear of God.

To fear God is also, as Michael Buckley puts it, to let God "contradict the programs and expectations of human beings in order to fulfill human desires and human freedom at a much deeper level than subjectivity would have measured out in its projections."[25] To fear God means to set aside our own expectations, needs, and imaginings and let God set the agenda and define the limits.

A healthy fear of God brings with it a sense that must flow over into our actions, that our freedom is not unconditional but conscienced. When we fear God, we fear misusing our freedom, not because we fear God's punishment if we do wrong, but because we fear hurting others, being idolatrous, or feeling self-righteous.

To live in holy fear of God means bringing one's freedom under the Lordship of God. One lives in holy fear of God when one is aware that freedom is a gift given us *for* love and that, outside its continual genuflection before a God beyond itself, freedom very quickly becomes a god unto itself and leaves in its wake a trail of violation, idolatry, and self-inflation. In Karl Rahner's words: "How often I have found out that we grow to maturity not by doing what we like, but by doing what we should. How true it is that not every *should* is a compulsion, and not every *like* is a high morality and true freedom."[26]

Lastly, a healthy fear of God means living in genuine

humility. This is not to be confused with timidity, shyness, introversion, or a bad self-image. The self-depreciating person who protests that he cannot do the job or should not be asked to lead is not necessarily the most humble. Self-depreciation and hesitation may be the product of a bad self-image or a natural introversion and timidity, and not the product of healthy humility.

The word *humility* comes from the Latin root *humus,* which means soil or earth. To be humble is to be earthy, not to be disconnected or have your head in the clouds, and to feel your dependence and interconnectedness with others and with the earth. It is to have a felt sense of your creatureliness, that is, of your limits and your vulnerability. The humblest person you know is not the person who lives a timid life but the person who lives a life that constantly acknowledges its interconnectedness and its radical incarnate character.

In our humility we recognize that we are a child of the earth, that we are dust. The fear of always losing our awareness of those connections is a holy fear, one which we owe to God, to each other, to the earth, and to ourselves.

Let God Be Your Justification

Each of us aches for significance, meaning, uniqueness, preciousness, immortality, and great love and great beauty in our lives. This yearning is congenital and incurable. We are, as Plato said, fired into life with this divine restlessness in us. But our madness comes, as Alan Jones says, when the pressure for a cure for our mortality and insignificance gets too great and we fabricate the vital lie.[27] We try, through our own efforts, to create significance, uniqueness, and immortality for ourselves.

In the Protestant tradition, contemplation is the antithesis of this madness. We contemplate when we put our hearts, minds, and lives in the correct posture, when we resist our spontaneous urge to achieve these things for ourselves and, instead, let God give them to us. When we are driven by goals that would fabricate for us the vital lie, we degenerate into a greed in spirit and body that makes wonder and awe impossible. The posture of our minds, hearts, and lives is one of possessive clutching. In her insightful diaries, Etty Hillesum captures what is at stake here:

> Whenever I saw a beautiful flower, what I longed to do with it was press it to my heart, or eat it all up. It was more difficult with a piece of beautiful scenery, but the feeling was the same. I was too sensual, I might almost write too greedy. I yearned physically for all I thought was beautiful, wanted to own it. Hence that painful longing that could never be satisfied, the pining for something I thought unattainable, which I called my creative urge. I believe it was this powerful emotion that made me think that I was born to produce great works. It all suddenly changed, God alone knows by what inner process, but it is different now. I realized it only this morning, when I recalled my short walk round the Skating Club a few nights ago. It was dusk, soft hues in the sky, mysterious silhouettes of houses, trees alive with the light through the tracery of their branches, in short, enchanting. And then I knew

precisely how I had felt in the past. Then all the beauty would have gone like a stab to my heart and I would not have known what to do with the pain. Then I would have felt the need to write, to compose verses, but the words would still have refused to come. I would have felt utterly miserable, wallowed in the pain and exhausted myself as a result. The experience would have sapped all my energy. Now I know it for what it was: mental masturbation.

Where talk and concern center around money, food, entertainment, sports, sex, and health, there is little sense that the earth is ablaze with the fire of God, and even less of a sense that one should have his shoes off before it.

But that night, only just gone, I reacted quite differently. I felt that God's world was beautiful despite everything, but its beauty now filled me with joy. I was just as deeply moved by that mysterious, still landscape in the dusk as I might have been before, but somehow I no longer wanted to own it. I went home invigorated and got to work. And the scenery stayed with me, in the background, as a cloak about my soul, to put it poetically for once, but it no longer held me back: I no longer "masturbated" with it.[28]

Hillesum is precisely describing contemplation. As long as she attempted to *own* beauty, the result was obsessive pain, constant restlessness, deep narcissism, and no sense of God. Conversely, once she stopped trying to take beauty to herself to assure her own beauty and meaning, she was able to see it with the sheer gaze of admiration.

After God told Moses to take off his shoes before the burning bush, Moses asked him: "What is your name?" God answered: *"Yahweh . . . I am who am."*[29] This name does not mean, as medieval commentators suggested, "I am the Being of Beings, the Ground of Being, or the one who causes everything that is." What it does mean is something less metaphysical, more personal, and directly significant for what it means to live contemplatively: *I am who am* refers to God's freedom, transcendence, and holiness. God's answer to Moses might be stated: "I am the one who cannot be encountered in thought, imagination, or feeling; the one who can never be controlled or manipulated; but who, despite this and because of it, is ever graciously and powerfully present to you. Trust that presence, walk in it, undergo it."

Where talk and concern centers around money, food, entertainment, sports, sex, and health, there is little sense that the earth is ablaze with the fire of God, and even less of a sense that one should have his shoes off before it. In our normal consciousness, whenever we approach God, even in formal prayer and in our churches, it is with very measured expectations. The God who is met in the measured expectations of our own desires and imagination dies in his own impotence and irrelevance.

Notes

1. Annie Dillard, *Holy the Firm* (New York, 1977), p. 59.

2. Isaiah 55:8-9.

3. Job 38–40.

4. Romans 1–8.

5. This is a paraphrase of G. K. Chesterton, *The Everlasting Man,* pp. 26–28.

6. The Fourth Lateran Council (1215) taught that the difference between God and creature is always greater than are the similarities between them. "Inter creatorem et creaturam non potest tanta similitudo notari quin inter eos major sit dissimilitudo notanda" (Denzinger-Banwart, *Enchiridion,* 11th ed., no. 432).

7. Isaiah 6:3.

8. Luke 15:11-32.

9. Matthew 20:1-16.

10. Luke 10:25-37.

11. John Shea, "The Indiscriminate Host," in *Stories of Faith* (Chicago, 1980), p. 175.

12. Harold Kushner, *When Bad Things Happen to Good People* (Indianapolis: Bobbs-Merrill, 1961).

13. R. Rubenstein, reflecting upon the unparalleled sin and inhumanity of Auschwitz, comments: "When I say we live in a time of the death of God, I mean that the thread uniting God and man, heaven and earth, has been broken. We stand in a cold, silent, unfeeling cosmos, unaided by any purposeful power beyond our own resources. After Auschwitz, what else can a Jew say about God, except that he is dead?" *After Auschwitz* (Indianapolis, 1966), p. 49.

14. Romans 1–8.

15. Alan Jones, *Journey into Christ* (New York, 1977), p. 57.

16. Quoted by Jürgen Moltmann, *The Crucified God* (London, 1974), p. 36.

17. See statement of the Fourth Lateran Council, note 6, above.

18. Exodus 3:1-6.

19. A paraphrase of Elizabeth Barrett Browning.

20. Henri Nouwen, *In Memoriam* (Notre Dame, Ind., 1980), pp. 27–30.

21. John Shea, *Stories of God,* p. 137.

22. Mark 13:28.

23. Job 40:3-5 and 42:1-3 (Jerusalem Bible translation).

24. G. K. Chesterton, *Everlasting Man*, p. 159.

25. Michael Buckley, "Atheism and Contemplation," pp. 696–97.

26. Karl Rahner, *Prayers for a Lifetime* (New York, 1989), p. 30.

27. Alan Jones, *Journey into Christ*, p. 57.

28. Etty Hillesum, *An Interrupted Life: The Diaries of Etty Hillesum, 1941–1943* (New York, 1981), p. 13.

29. Exodus 3:13-14.

six

Recognizing and Appropriating the Experience of Contingency

The Philosophical Tradition of Theism

Proofs for the Existence of God

It suffices for things to exist for God to become inevitable. Accord to a point of moss, to the smallest ant, the value of existence, and we cannot escape any longer from the terrifying hands which move us all.[1]

Jacques Maritain's words capture the central idea of a school of contemplative thought that is commonly referred to as classical theism. Its central belief is that God is only dead when, in our ordinary lives, we lose the awareness of our own contingency, that is, of our radical dependence on something beyond ourselves.

As we've seen, when Nietzsche said that God is dead he was speaking about the death of God in human awareness and not about whether God actually exists. Our spontaneous consciousness is normally unaware of his existence. In a normal day, with all our heartaches and headaches, God is generally absent to us.

Classical theism takes this position; that, for the most part, God is dead in our day-to-day consciousness. This is not because no God exists to be known, or because our ordinary experience is secular and God can be found only in explicit religious experience (prayer and church). It is because we do not perceive our own secular experience properly since we are focused on only one dimension of that experience. If we were fully awake to what is contained in our so-called secular experience, we would find that God is far from dead. Classical theism believes that God is the ground, horizon, and author of our every experience. Classical theism is very similar to the mystical tradition and, for that reason, merits being designated as a contemplative tradition. The difference between them is that classical theists take a philosophical, abstract, and descriptive approach rather than a religious, pious, and prescriptive one. Classical theism believes that, at every second, we and everything in our universe are being actively breathed into existence and held by God. If God stopped actively creating for one second, we and everything in the universe would disappear into nothingness. Imagine a dancer dancing. The dance exists only while it is being danced by the dancer. The instant the dancer stops, the dance ceases. This tradition understands human life and all creation in the same way. We are God's dance.

Contemplative perception—being wide awake to all that is revealed in our experience—shows us that, in Austin Farrer's words, when we perceive correctly, we see . . . :

> not *the-creature-without-the-creator*
> or *the-creator-without-the-creature*

but *the-creature-and-the-creator-in-the-cosmologi-cal relationship.*[2]

When we see contemplatively we perceive every-thing against a divine horizon. Or, as Thomas Aquinas put it, when we see correctly, we recognize contingency, and when we recognize contingency, we have proof for the existence of God.

═════════════ ❧ ═════════════

If we were fully awake to what is contained
in our so-called secular experience, we would
find that God is far from dead.

The proponents of this idea are usually associated with philosophy rather than religion, and they repre-sent a wide variety of backgrounds and historical peri-ods: Anselm, Thomas Aquinas, Leibnitz, Spinoza, René Descartes, Emmanuel Kant, Etienne Gilson, William Paley, Austin Farrer, Jacques Maritain, Eric Mascall, Jan Walgrave, Martin D'Arcy, Bernard Lonergan, Karl Rah-ner, Paul Tillich, Charles Hartshorne, Langdon Gilkey, Peter Berger, and Joseph Marechal, among others. Some of them have been associated with what has been com-monly called "the proofs for existence of God"; others have not. Despite immense differences in their thought, they are part of one tradition in that all of them affirm that proper perception reveals, however inchoately, the sense that ordinary experience is grounded in God.

They express this in many different ways and, in nearly all cases, abstractly. In fact, their ideas are often considered too abstract even for minds trained in philosophy to grasp. We will attempt to step outside the language of technical philosophy and explain what members of this school call "rumors of angels" or "traces of ultimacy" in ordinary experience.

How and where does a divine horizon manifest itself in ordinary experience?

The Argument from the Outside . . . Proofs for the Existence of God

Bernard Lonergan once made the statement that all proofs for the existence of God can be reduced to a single premise: If reality is intelligible, then God exists![3] Throughout the centuries, many philosophers have developed elaborate arguments to prove that God exists. Their arguments vary greatly, but, in the end, all of them are based on the same premise: if the world makes sense then some ultimate principle—God—must exist to explain it.

One such argument was made by the English philosopher William Paley, in a book entitled *Natural Theology: Evidence of the Deity Collected from Appearances of Nature,* which was published in 1802. He argued as follows. You are walking down a road when your foot accidentally strikes a stone. You ask: "Who put this stone here? Was it always here? Does it need anything beyond itself to explain itself?" As far as you are concerned the stone could have been there forever. The stone of itself does not force you to think further about it. Now, in a slightly different scene, you are walking along a road when your foot accidentally bumps into a watch. It is ticking and has the correct time. You ask: "Who put this watch here? Was it always here? Does it need anything beyond itself to explain itself?" In this case, our minds will not allow us the simple answer, that the watch has been lying there forever and that nobody left it there. Why not? Because it is ticking (if it had been there forever it would already have stopped ticking) and because it a deliberate design that demands that a certain intelligence built it (blind chance might make stones, but it does not construct watches).

Paley tells us to look at the design in our world and especially at the design in ourselves. The human body, with its brain and central nervous system, is such an incredible entity of intelligent and deliberate design that one cannot look at it and say, as one might in the case of a stone, that it does not need anything beyond itself to be here. The intelligent purposeful design of the human body, heart, and mind demand a different answer, require something beyond themselves to explain their existence. That something has to be a reality that itself is not contingent on anything else. It must be the ground of all intelligence, purpose, and existence. In a word, it must be God.

This is the argument from contingency, expressed by many different thinkers in many different ways: things as we know them do not fully explain themselves. In the end, only some Ultimate, God, can account for the simple fact of existence.

Moreover, these proofs suggest something that is apropos to contemplation. According to this tradition, when we perceive things properly, we see them against this background of ultimacy. Thus, you cannot see a watch without knowing at the same time that there is a watchmaker; you cannot see a dance without seeing at the same time a dancer; you cannot see a creature without also knowing the creator; and you cannot be properly aware of who you really are—a being who does not account for its own existence—without knowing at some level that there is an Ultimate being that does account for your existence. You cannot be fully perceiving and feeling if you are unaware that some Ultimate exists as a ground for all that is.

These proofs are not equations that bind the intellect the way a mathematical formula does. They are not demonstrations to the human intellect; they are "monstrations to contemplative intellection."[4] What does this curious phrase mean?

The Christian creeds are a set of formulae which of themselves do not prove that Christ was divine, that he rose from the dead, and that there is eternal life. They function not as proof, but as a truth and a challenge to Christian consciousness as it journeys adventurously through history not to veer from the whole truth, to avoid a narrowed or incomplete consciousness of Christ. A Christian who finds herself at variance with the creeds must do serious self-examination. The proofs for the existence of God function in a parallel fashion. A person whose everyday consciousness is experienced as purely secular must ask himself some hard questions: "Am I optimally open? How pure or cloudy is my awareness? Am I too preoccupied with certain things and unaware of others? Am I missing the forest for the trees . . . the watchmaker for the watch . . . the dancer for the dance . . . the wide horizon for the narrow perspective . . . and the Ultimate for the finite? When I no longer see something is it because it is not there or because I am not present?"

The classical proofs for the existence of God are useful as an invitation and guide to contemplation. According to this tradition, just as Christ left us the invitation to "recognize him in the breaking of the bread," our very existence invites us perennially to recognize God in our lack of self-sufficiency. This, however, becomes clearer when, in a sense, we turn the arguments inside out so as to see what they *feel* like rather than look like.

The Argument from the Inside . . . Theism as an Invitation to Contemplation

The proponents of classical theism assure us that ordinary experience offers constant proofs for the existence of God, and that there is no such thing as purely secular experience. Why are we not more aware of this? Why does our experience feel perennially and pathologically secular? Why do we not see the creator when we see the creature?

Classical theism's simple answer to these questions is that there is a fault in contemplation. God is there to be seen; we just fail to see properly. There are traces of ultimacy in ordinary experience; we stop short of appropriating them. We do, in fact, even *feel* God; we are just not aware enough of what we are feeling.

They distinguish between non-contemplative awareness and contemplative awareness, what we are normally conscious of in our experience and what really exists in our actual experience when it is examined in all its complexity and totality.

When we view our experience non-contemplatively it appears to us, save for very rare instances, as secular, that is, it does not point beyond itself to the existence of God, nor does it contain "traces of ultimacy," "rumors of angels," "hierophanies," "contuitions of God," or "a divine horizon." Conversely, when we view our experience contemplatively, it infallibly brings us to see beyond the dance to the Dancer. It always yields a contuition of God. Experience, classical theists contend, examined under the light of a proper hermeneutics, is never secular. We can feel secular only if we are not really in touch with what we are experiencing.

What do we actually feel in our ordinary lives? Do we *feel* God's presence in our ordinary awareness? Is there no purely secular experience? Contemporary theists like Langdon Gilkey and Peter Berger, among others, submit that we do not *feel* all that secular, and that our ordinary experience is always affected by a sense of something beyond it, some ultimate that relativizes it.

They illustrate this by analyzing how the major characteristics of the so-called secular mindset are felt by contemporary people. They suggest that there is a huge difference between what we commonly *profess* to experience and what we *actually* do experience. Our secular version of what is contained in our experience is, not unlike our opinion about ourselves, often quite different from the facts. We do not, in fact, experience ourselves as secular, that is, without a god, without absolutes, mortal, and under no obligation of obedience to something higher than ourselves—as the creed of secularity would have us believe. Our experience reveals something quite different.

Secular Experience Seen Non-Contemplatively

The so-called secular mindset, in its self-understanding, defines itself by four major characteristics, contingency, relativity, transience, and autonomy.

The secular mindset would have us believe that the immediate is all that there is, that existence begins and ends with the here and now. In this view, the human person and the cosmos are not the result of a deliberate and loving act of a God, nor does it have any ultimate principle of purpose, order, or coherence. Beyond the here and now, there lies nothing—no explanation, no reason, no final plan or purpose. Existence just is.

Langdon Gilkey aptly summarizes this position. Secularism sees us as "set within a universe with neither a transcendent source nor an inherent or ultimate order; our nature is constituted exhaustively by blind nature or a meaningless void, not hostile, to be sure, but empty of purpose, indifferent, a faceless mystery. We can talk about it only in terms of the immediately given patterns of our phenomenal experience of it; beyond that we can know and speak nothing about what is."[5] George Santayana expresses the same idea poetically: "Matter is the invisible wind which, sweeping for no reason over the field of essences, raises some of them into a cloud of dust: and that whirlwind we call existence . . . and, in such a world, necessity is a conspiracy of accidents."[6]

Another aspect of the secular mindset is that we experience our existence as relative, that is, we find nothing absolute. There are no unconditional oughts. All our experience is pinioned to the flow of change and history, determined by what lies behind it, shaped by what surrounds it, and replaced by what follows it. Everything in our universe is essentially interrelated and must be understood in terms of the nexus of relationships out of which it has been formed, rather than in relationship to anything transcendent to it. There is nothing outside of nature and history, nothing that is underived, unchanging, and self-sufficient.

Another key prong of the secular mindset is that we experience ourselves and everything else as mortal and transient. Secular experience affirms that all is in time and is due to die. Nothing will last, all is time-bound between birth and death. Accordingly, the relevant environment for our hopes and fears is confined to this life. Concepts such as "forever," "next life," "eternity," and "kingdom of God beyond history" have no meaning; they are seen as expressions of wishful thinking.

Proponents of secularity also believe that, except for a certain guilt neurosis that many of us carry over from our religious past, we are free to shape our lives according to our own choices for meaning as opposed to being obligated to live out a form of obedience to a God above us. We are, they say, self-creative, meant to decide for ourselves the meaning of existence. Values are not lived out because of the wishes or plan of a transcendent deity, or because we are given a vocation from something antecedent to ourselves that we respect and submit ourselves to, but because we have freely chosen them to give meaning to our lives. We are our own project, called to creativity, not obedience.

Obedience, submission, and self-surrender to something above us or beyond us is seen as either as naivete or weakness in the face of the truth of our condition. We are on our own, and there is no need to refer our behavior to courts above our own. There is often a certain aggressiveness towards anything that suggests a lack of free choice. The suggestion that one must be obedient to a transcendent God, or to a transcendent norm, is an affront to the contemporary mindset.

The ideology of secularism would have us believe that our ordinary experience of this world is all that there is. It alone is relevant in terms of hope, purpose, moral choice, and fulfillment. There are no absolutes, there is no forever. We wake up in this world as orphans. There is no great creator who can help us and to whom we owe obedience. Our lives are shaped *only* by the accidents of history, the web of our interrelationships, what this life can offer, and the meaning we can give ourselves through our free choices.

Some proponents of secularity view this positively and optimistically, as an opportunity to be free of the asphyxiating dictates of a non-existent God and his very existent clerics. This worldview confers a chance to come of age, to grow up. Others, such as Albert Camus, view this negatively. If there is no God, we are pathetically abandoned, and robbed of deep meaning, final significance, and the ultimate loving graciousness which alone vindicates love and makes life worth living. In either case, however, the bottom line is the same: we are contingent, relative, transient, and on our own.

Is this the true picture? Do we experience ourselves and the world in this way?

Secular Experience Seen Contemplatively

Classical theism asserts that the philosophy of secularism is not true. Ordinary experience, classical theism assures us, is full of hierophanies, and traces of transcendence. God is anything but dead.

Contingency Revisited

They turn, armed with a hermeneutical flashlight, to reexamine the ideas of secularism.

───────────── ╰╮ ─────────────

For secularism, there are no absolutes,
there is no forever. We wake up in this
world as orphans.

─────────────────────────────────

When we examine our own experience, at one level it seems that this world and all it offers are all that is real and important, that any purpose and meaning we give our lives must be taken from the here and now, which is the relevant sphere for our hopes. At another level, though, our actual experience belies that impression. In nearly all of our ordinary actions, we experience something beyond the purely immediate. Much to our own consternation at times, we find ourselves facing something much larger than the finite. This is experienced either as the ultimate threat or the ultimate benevolence.

It is experienced negatively when we have feelings of helplessness, dependency, emptiness, terror, void, and threat that are entirely out of proportion to our immediate experience. Unlike neurosis and other obsessions that can also trigger deep feelings of void beyond what the present situation merits, this experience is marked by its character of ultimacy. It does not just cause deep pain in one area, it totally relativizes everything and leaves us with the feeling that the here and now is flimsy and unimportant. There is a dim sense that there is something beyond, something whose reality dwarfs the present.

If we believe that there is nothing, no God, no ultimate foundation, no meaning to existence, then nothingness itself takes on the character of the ultimate and forces our horizon beyond the here and now. An infinite void becomes the god before which everything we are and do is threatened in an ultimate way. God is experienced not as a first and final principle that creates and sustains us, but as a threat that can extinguish us. Nonetheless, there is the sense of something absolute in such an experience.

This experience is not uncommon and is had by people of all ages. We use expressions such as "keeping the demons at bay" to describe it. Few and lucky are those who never find their ordinary lives, either in their waking hours and in their dreams, terrorized by the sense of standing before an absolute void.

Confronted by such a threat, we inevitably search desperately for some positive ultimate, a gracious god who can steady our lives. We then either find God, create idols, or end up in despair. Ordinary existence, entirely independent of any explicit religious considerations, forces that choice on us—God or despair! We are unable to live merrily for very long on the basis of the here and now. Absolute void and absolute graciousness consistently subvert our attempts to live, love, and hope on the basis of the immediate. Without being invited in, some god inevitably casts a threatening shadow or a gracious light into our present moment. For this reason, we never have a purely secular experience.

The positive side of this is experienced in bursts of life that are inexplicable purely in terms of the here and now. In our day-to-day experience, there is present, as the very foundation of all we are and do, a sense of joy, vitality, meaning, and strength that is only explicable by something beyond the immediate. Unless we are clinically depressed, we always have the sense that our lives and the universe are good and have meaning because, at their deepest level, they are buoyed up and continually refuelled by some ultimate gracious power.

This is something we feel more than think. It manifests itself unconsciously in our vitality and in our valuing of persons, things, and ourselves. It manifests itself, in a word, as health. We have the feeling, no matter how dimly, that it is good to be alive. As Langdon Gilkey puts it:

> We all love our own being, our existence, our life. Humans are aware of many joys, of course, but underneath all of them there is the exultation in being alive, in feeling and using one's powers—of sensing, smelling, eating, loving, using one's body. Here we experience the sheer joy of being and existing: here the reality and power of *existence* are felt from the inside as joyful vitality. And this inner and most vital joy is the center and ground of all valuing; it provides the most basic reason for existing, though it is much more a fundamental tone to our being in the world than it is a rational reason.[7]

This sense of the goodness of existence is experienced as as a gift, uncreated by ourselves.

The sociologist of religion Peter Berger gives an excellent illustration.

> Consider the most ordinary, and probably the most fundamental, of all—the ordinary gesture by which a mother reassures her anxious child.
>
> A child wakes up in the night, perhaps from a bad dream, and finds himself surrounded by darkness, alone, beset by nameless threats. At such a moment the contours of trusted reality are blurred and invisible. In the terror of incipient chaos the child cries out for his mother. It is hardly an exaggeration to say that, at this moment, the mother is being invoked as a high priestess of protective order. It is she (and, in many cases, she alone) who has the power to banish the chaos and to restore the benign shape of the world. And, of course, any good mother will do just that. She will take the child and cradle him in the timeless gesture of the Magna Mater who became our Madonna. She will turn on a lamp, perhaps, which will encircle the scene with a warm glow of reassuring light. She will speak or sing to the child and the content of this communication will invariably be the same—"Don't be afraid—everything is in order, everything is all right."[8]

The mother's comforting reassurance is, in fact, a profession of faith. Although not explicitly, she is saying: "I believe in God, the Almighty, the creator of heaven and earth who made existence good and whose love and

redemptive power will, in the end, assure that goodness
. . . and so you can trust!"

When she reassures the child that there is nothing to
be frightened about, she means it not so much on the
basis that there are no immediate dangers to the child,
as on the basis that, *ultimately,* we are all in the hands of
graciousness and love and not in the hands of mali-
ciousness and terror. She believes this not on the basis of
any explicit religious consideration, but on the basis of
something *given* to her along with her ordinary perception and awareness—namely, the sense that, in the end,
everything is all right because the dance of creation is
being danced by an all-good and all-loving Dancer.

---

*The mother's comforting reassurance is,
in fact, a profession of faith.*

Classical theism submits that this is what ordinary
experience reveals when it is flushed out by the beam of
a good hermeneutical flashlight, or by proper contemplativeness. Far from finding that the secular world is
the relevant environment for our hopes, we find instead
that there is no neutral middle ground on which to
experience it without ultimate graciousness or ultimate
void invading it. Unlike animals, we are not afforded the
opportunity to munch our food contentedly and be
happy or restless on that basis. Our ordinary lives are
buoyed up or damped down by hope or despair that
have their roots in something deeper and more fundamental than what is contained in the immediate.
Whether we feel at any given minute that everything is

all right or not all right depends more upon what traces of ultimacy we are experiencing than upon what is superficially present to us in that moment.

Ordinary awareness is not so ordinary.

Relativity Revisited

Secularism would have us believe that nothing presents itself to us as absolute, eternal, permanent, and non-negotiable. Classical theism submits that our true experience reveals the opposite, that in our lives, and habitually so, we find that we cannot make decisions, motivate ourselves, or find meaning except by relating to an absolute.

Animals live largely by instinct. They do not have to struggle for meaning. For them, meaning comes from biological programming.

In humans, biological instinct is much weaker and we must live and find meaning beyond our genetic programming. We choose actions and consciously design patterns of behavior. For our lives to have meaning, we behave in such a way that our actions are not merely a succession of events related only by chance and accident, but construct a meaningful *pattern* of behavior. When there is no pattern to our actions we experience meaninglessness.

For this to occur, for there to be a meaningful pattern, there must be one thread that somehow our actions to each other and dyes them all with a common color of meaning. We grab this thread by connecting ourselves to an end, a destiny that we sense will give us ultimate meaning. From this *telos,* we draw the string backwards and, anchored to our final destiny, it binds all our actions into one meaningful whole. If the thread breaks, or if the end point shifts or is no longer considered absolute, we have a crisis of meaning.

We cannot live meaningfully without a teleology—a higher purpose or goal—and we create a teleology for ourselves *only* by relating to an absolute anchor. Secular experience is not, it seems, so secular after all. We find that, irrespective of explicit religious commitment, we live our lives always in relationship to an absolute.

Freud once said that we understand the anatomy of things best if we look at them when they are broken. With this in mind, it is interesting to look at what happens when someone tries to live without absolutes.

We see a poignant illustration of this in Albert Camus's novel *L'Étranger*.[9] Meursault, the anti-hero, is a young man who works as a clerk in Algiers. He lives in the usual manner of a young middle-class bachelor: cooking his own meals, sleeping with his girlfriend, holidaying at weekends, drinking with his friends, reading and going to the cinema. But, since he does not believe in God, he cannot find a reason to do anything, including loving or hating. He judges everything to be relative and has no meaning in his life. All his actions are performed in complete indifference. When his girlfriend asks him, "Do you love me?" he answers that he supposes he doesn't but that, in any case, the question is meaningless. When she asks whether he would consent to marry her, he answers that he does not care one way or the other, but he would marry her if she would like that. He eventually kills a man, without passion or hatred and even without any good reason for it. He is condemned to be executed and faces his death with indifference. Nothing—living, loving, dying, helping friends, or the death of a family member—is a matter of more than comfort or inconvenience.

We all know that, barring some rare depressed or stoic exceptions, nobody lives with the indifference of Camus's *L'Étranger*. Irrespective of explicit belief in God, most people create for themselves a teleology that holds their lives together, motivates them, gives them a sense of purpose and destiny, and incites them to love and hate with some zest.

When we examine the teleologies we create, we find that the absolute that we connect our destiny and meaning to becomes the normative criterion against which all value is measured. Many people, for example, while rejecting any explicit belief in God or any other absolute, invariably set up certain ideals as normative—political, cultural, moral, humanitarian, educational, aesthetic— and then invest these ideals with an absoluteness that mimics and parallels every movement of religion, including the accusation of sacrilege against anyone who treats with irreverence what is cherished as sacred. (For example, Marxism idealizes personal development, social justice, sexual fulfillment, concern for the environment, and the health of one's body.) These ideals, which invariably become ideologies and idols, are surrogate gods and functions as the anchor for the thread that gives life meaning.

We need to refer ourselves to an absolute not just as motivation, but to provide the proper symbolic hedge around our actions.

Waiting is an essential and characteristic part of life. We live habitually in restlessness, unfulfilled, yearning, unconsummated, waiting for someone or something to arrive that will fulfill us. Normally, this tension can be endured and is part of a hope we live with, a hope that we have a destiny that will eventually come about. Waiting is a meaningful activity because we do it under a certain symbolic hedge; there is, in fact, something to wait for. We experience the flow of time meaningfully, despite our tension and incompleteness.

But when we are deprived of a reference to an absolute, waiting becomes absurd and loses all meaning. This is brilliantly illustrated by Samuel Beckett in his play *Waiting for Godot.*

=============== 🌿 ===============

Many people, while rejecting any explicit belief in God or any other absolute, invariably set up certain ideals as normative—and then invest these ideals with an absoluteness that mimics and parallels every movement of religion.

The play centers on two old tramps, Vladimir and Estragon, who are waiting for a Mr. Godot, with whom they vaguely believe themselves to have an appointment. It is evident that Mr. Godot is never going to arrive. Their waiting, since it has no ultimate purpose, is pointless and absurd. Time weighs heavy, and becomes a meaningless burden.

What Samuel Beckett illustrates is first cousin to what Camus depicts in *L'Étranger:* without reference to an absolute, life cannot be rendered meaningful. For Camus's Meursault, there is nothing that can ultimately motivate him; for Beckett's stood-up tramps, there is no meaningful way to pass the time. For classical theism, this is what the proofs for the existence of God *feel* like when they are turned inside out and upside down. The doctrine of the absurdity of the world is what the doctrine of the contingency of the world becomes when it is transposed from a theistic to an atheistic setting.

What is true for the experience of waiting is also true for the experience of sexuality. All understandings of sexuality that strip away its teleological and symbolic hedge and reduce it to a here and now experience devoid of the dimensions of ultimacy and sacredness, render it ambiguous and depreciate what it has to offer. When sexual encounter is not related, however inchoately, to ultimate destiny and meaning, it remains pleasurable, as does eating a good meal, but it loses much of its power to trigger depth and create union beyond fleeting sensation.

Doris Lessing explores this theme brilliantly in her five-volume series on Martha Quest. Her heroine rejects belief in God and, save for brief periods of her life, anything else with dimensions of ultimacy and sacredness. Her ensuing struggle to find a teleology that binds her life into a meaningful whole is extremely enlightening, particularly as she struggles to find meaning in her sexuality. For Martha, sex does not point to anything beyond itself; accordingly, it loses all reference to destiny, depth, significance, and, at last, even to love.

> Sex: sensation pulsing on the current of blood and breath. Heartbeat-heart: separate. Heart with emotions, "love," but isolated and looked at like this, a small thing, a pulse of little feeling, like an animal impulse towards another, a

warmth. Sex, heart, the currents of the automatic body. . . .

She understood that it was this that had sent Mark up to Martha to make love. What an extraordinary phrase that was, "make love." Love, love . . . Martha sat listening, while the word "love" exploded and bred, and thought of the act in which she had engaged so very many times and with different people: she could see Martha, in different shapes, and sizes, according to the time, her limbs moving, enlaced with this man, that man, always the same way, or so it looked from where she was now, but subjectively, putting herself back inside the act, it was not possible to use the same words for what she felt. Mark, when he had come upstairs, possessed by some explosive force which gripped her now, and had made love, made sex, made something, had used a different energy from what Jack had used, all that time ago when he used their two bodies like conductors or conduits for the force which moved and lifted them to—she could not remember where. . . . She was sitting and muttering as she had years before: We don't understand the first thing about what goes on, not the first thing, "make love," "make sex," "orgasms," "climaxes"—it was all nonsense, words, sounds, invented by half-animals who understood nothing at all. Great forces as impersonal as thunder or lightning or sunlight or the movement of oceans being contracted and heaved and rolled in their beds by the moon, swept through bodies, and now she knew quite well why Mark had come blindly upstairs to the nearest friendly body, being in the grip of this force or *a* force, one of them. Not sex. Not necessarily. Not unless one chose to make it so.

Jack had once said: "The thousand volts." He had been talking of hate. "The thousand volts of hatred." A thousand volts of love? A thousand volts of—compassion? Of charity?[10]

We see that sexuality, like existence itself, cannot be rendered meaningful unless, within it, there is an awareness of a connection to some absolute. Like Camus and Beckett, Lessing shows that unless we grasp "the-dance-in-relationship-to-the-Dancer" we are unable to make much sense of the dance.

An obvious objection can be raised here, namely that of Feuerbach and Marx: the fact that we cannot find meaning in life without reference to an absolute does not mean such an absolute exists. Proving that we would want and need a God is not the same thing as proving that a God exists.

That critique, however valid in many other contexts, misses a critical point in the argument here. These examples illustrate not that we need a God, but that we function spontaneously in the light of the fact that we have already apprehended one. The totally *a-theistic* characters of Camus, Beckett, and Lessing are the ones who are strained and contrived, not the sense that we and our actions are related to some absolute. The Martha Quests, Meursaults, Vladimirs and Estragons exist more in the pages of literature and philosophy than in real life, where there is the congenital inability to accept meaninglessness for very long.

Transience Revisited

Our actual experience comes laden with dimensions that make a tranquil acceptance of mortality impossible. Our felt existence belies our espoused beliefs: We live meaningful lives by not accepting mortality and transience. We refuse death at its every turn.

So much of what we do derives from the drive for immortality. We cannot stand the knowledge that we are merely animals that live and die and that, in the end, death and insignificance is our lot. In our depths there is something that radically rejects this, and we act accordingly. We attempt to guarantee immortality for ourselves: set a world record, become famous, have a child, write a book. In each of us there is the compulsion to leave a permanent mark.

Moreover, even as we say the words "Someday I will die!" we do not really accept them. We have a death-denying mechanism inside us that blocks out the fact of our own death. Others around us die from accidents, cancer, disease, old age, but death takes others, never us. Even as we one part of us knows that we will die, another part of us knows that it is not true.

We refuse, too, to accept, at any point in our olives, that our lives are as good as they will ever get. Our minds and hearts, unconsciously and consciously, refuse to acknowledge the limits of our growth and development. Even when we are (in the literal sense of that colloquial expression) "over the hill," in terms of our practical hopes, we know at some other level that we are not. We are sure that in terms of real life that we are still babies and that what we yearn to attain in terms of love, creativity, achievement, and significance is still in our future. Never do we accept any present as the highest, most significant, healthiest, and happiest moment we will ever experience.

Most radically, though, we experience our refusal of death in our experience of hope. We possess an astonishing capacity to hope in the face of any situation, no matter how hopeless it is. Even when we are surrounded by death, our inmost being says a resounding *No* to death in a most radical way. We affirm life and ultimate graciousness despite how awful our concrete historical situation might be. A powerful example of this can be seen in the words that a prisoner about to be executed by the Nazis during the Second World War wrote on a concentration camp wall:

> I believe in the sun, even when it isn't shining.
> I believe in love, even when I feel it not.
> I believe in God, even when he is silent.

On what basis do we humans possess this stunning ability to affirm graciousness and love as the heart of reality when the here and now demands the opposite affirmation?

The answer to that can only be that somehow we apprehend in the here and now—despite its often brutal suggestion that death and darkness are the final answer—a gracious absolute that lies beyond. Like the classical theist who looks at a rose and is able to perceive the creator and sustainer who gives it existence at that precise moment, so too do we sense the gracious Dancer who is Lord over all dances, including the horrible one that now threatens us, and who will bring us all to a new day and a new loving dance.

Autonomy Revisited

Do we really believe that we no longer need to submit to a transcendent being to whom we owe obedience in holy fear? Does the human person today, as the non-contemplative ideology of secularism contends, feel confident to create his own meaning, independent of a transcendent will? Do we really feel liberated, free, autonomous, no longer under the dominion of a God?

We affirm life and ultimate graciousness despite how awful our concrete historical situation might be.

When we examine our actual feelings and behavior we see a huge difference between the ideology that proclaims our autonomy and our actual felt experience. In real life, we experience our freedom as conditioned by some absolute lord who, while demanding obedience, promises redemption.

We experience our freedom as ambiguous and flawed. Like Paul, sensitive people experience freedom as something they are not fully in control of. They know that they need redemption for moral impotence and failings. As Paul said, "I cannot understand my own behavior. I fail to carry out the things I want to do, and find myself doing the very things I hate . . . with the result that instead of doing the good things I want to do, I carry out the sinful things I do not want."[11]

There is a universal ring to those words. All people know that there are insoluble and inexplicable levels of complexity, hypocrisy, and moral impotence inside them that render them incapable much of the time of living out their own ideals. Leonard Bernstein, in his *Mass*, poetically describes this feeling:

> What I say I don't feel
> What I feel I don't show
> What I show isn't real
> What is real, Lord—I don't know
> No, no, no—I don't know.
>
> I don't know why every time
> I find a new love I wind up destroying it
> I don't know why I'm
> So freaky-minded, I keep on kind of enjoying
>   it—
> Why I drift off to sleep
> With pledges of deep resolve again,
> Then along comes the day
> And suddenly they dissolve again—
> I don't know . . .
>
> What I need I don't have
> What I have I don't own
> What I own I don't want
> What I want, Lord, I don't know.[12]

Another expression of the flawed quality of human autonomy is found in the words of Anna Blaman:

> I realized that it is simply impossible for a human being to be and remain "good" or

"pure." If, for instance, I wanted to be attentive in one direction, it could only be at the cost of neglecting another. If I gave my heart to one thing, I left another in the cold . . . No day and no hour goes by without my being guilty of some inadequacy. We never do enough, and what we do is never well enough done . . . except being inadequate, which we are good at, because it is the way we are made. This is true of me and of everyone else. Every day and every hour brings with it its weight of moral guilt, as regards my work and relations with others . . . I am constantly catching myself out in my human failings, and in spite of their being implied in my human imperfections, I am conscious of a sort of check. And this means that my human shortcomings are also my human guilt. It sounds strange that we should be guilty where we can do nothing about it. But even where there is no purpose, or deliberate intention, we have a conviction of our own shortcomings, and of consequent guilt, a guilt which sometimes shows itself all too clearly in the consequences of what we have done or left undone.[13]

Neither St. Paul, Leonard Bernstein, and Anna Blaman are expressing neurosis, but sensitive renderings of a universal human experience—human freedom is partly mystery and cannot be rendered fully intelligible in purely secular terms. It needs the broken language of religion that ties autonomy to redemption, original sin, justification, grace, and atonement. Against these other realities our freedom can be rendered intelligible and lived with creatively. Devoid of them, autonomy becomes unintelligible and we become, in the words of existential philosophy, an absurdity. To live happily in freedom, we need a Redeemer

Our actual experience of freedom teaches us this daily. In the practice of our personal freedom we experience our radical dependence upon God and, more importantly, *already* experience, albeit inchoately, redemption by that God. In a paraphrase of Austin Farrer, we experience not the flawed character and ambiguity of freedom's dance, but the flawed character and ambiguity of freedom's dance being redeemed by an ultimately gracious Dancer.

We experience our freedom as conscienced, not as absolute or as arbitrary. We find ourselves always before a tribunal that is infinite, absolute, and personal, and that demands our obedience and worship. In fact, freedom is always experienced in relationship to some lord.

In Dan Berrigan's words, "I have been searching for years for someone to be obedient to. That is a conservative statement, a profoundly traditional one, and so I mean it. For I am persuaded, in Simone Weil's phrase, that obedience is a need of the soul; that, without proper scope and corrected shape and admonitory word, we languish and inflate and grow foolish, even to ourselves."[14]

Doris Lessing illustrates this in her *Golden Notebook*. Her heroine, Anna, tries in a serious way to live out the philosophy that the human person has come of age and is free of all need for obedience to anything transcendent. Anna is a very gifted writer. She also possesses intelligence, attractiveness, and money. Yet as she attempts to live as a fully liberated person, she senses that her personality is disintegrating and she cannot explain why. The book ends, as it begins, with Lessing asking: "It's all very odd, isn't it?"[15] Lessing submits that the human personality falls apart unless it finds some lord, however that might be conceived. Left on our own, without an absolute to which to relate, our lives become unintelligible and odd, even to ourselves.

Langdon Gilkey shows how the axiom "what is natural to us is not atheism but idolatry" is spontaneously played out in our contemporary world.[16] He points out how all of us, whether we admit it or not, serve some lord, a real or surrogate God. Our freedom finds itself unable to operate meaningfully without genuflecting before the absolute, be that Yahweh, Allah, Krishna, Brahmin, Mother Earth, an ideology, an astrological sign, the harmony of the planets, universal love, an aesthetic ideal, the beauty of the human body, the power of romance or sex, or a political, social, moral, or ecological cause. Everyone invests something with the attributes of God and then lives obediently to that lord and sacrifices and worships accordingly. As many a poet has put it, we find salvation in surrender.

Our freedom also spontaneously and habitually moves us towards worship. As Chesterton so aptly put it, we feel ourselves most truly free and human when we are kneeling in submission. Analyzing pagan worship, he writes:

> (There is) a thing very deep in humanity indeed. . . . This deep truth of the danger of insolence, or being too big for our boots, runs through all the great Greek tragedies and makes them great. . . .
> The crux and crisis is that we find it natural to worship; even natural to worship unnatural

things. The posture of the idol might be stiff and strange; but the gesture of worship is generous and beautiful. We not only feel freer when we bend, we actually feel taller when we bow. Henceforth anything that takes away the gesture of worship stunts and even maims us forever. Henceforth being merely secular is servitude and inhibition. If we cannot pray we are gagged; if we cannot kneel we are in iron.[17]

Chesterton adds that in the ordinary gesture of prayer, it is normal and necessary that our hands are lifted up, but, he contends, it is no less a parable that our hands are empty!

———————— 〽 ————————

When we see our lives correctly,
we see that all is gift.

We see therefore that the ordinary experience of freedom brings with it, however little this might be explicitly acknowledged, the propensity for obedience to and worship of some absolute. We are incurably conscienced, incurably drawn to self-surrender in obedience, and incurably drawn to worship. In our freedom, always, we sense ourselves as standing before a God. To again paraphrase Austin Farrer: we experience our free dance in relationship to the Lord of the dance . . . to whose rhythm we sense that we must adjust our steps!

We shall never become theists if we take the world for granted; but so long as we do not take

it for granted we are within measurable distance
of taking it as granted us by God.[18]

These words by Eric Mascall sum up the contemplative
praxis of classical theism. This school of thought can be
reduced to a single prescription: *Appropriate your contingency!* Be aware of what is gift in your life. Be alert to
and searingly honest in accepting all that you find present in your experience and you will find that you are
not a self-sufficient being but that at each second of
your life you are being created, sustained, challenged,
and redeemed by some absolute beyond you. When the
sense of gift is lost, we concomitantly experience the
death of the Giver!

At the end of Luke's gospel, Christ invites us to "recognize him in the breaking of the bread," in eucharist.
Eucharist means thanksgiving. Thanksgiving and gratitude follow upon the recognition of gift. Classical theism
as a contemplative tradition invites us to recognize God
in the experience of being given a gift (for that is what
contingency means). When we see our lives correctly, we
see that all is gift. If we appropriate this, then our eyes
will be opened and we will recognize that God has been
walking on the road with us all along. We will say to
each other, "were not our hearts burning within us as he
spoke to us through all those experiences that we felt
were only secular?"

Notes

1. Jacques Maritain, *The Degrees of Knowledge: Distinguish to Unite*
(ET, London, 1937), p. 132.

2. Austin Farrer, *Finite and Infinite: A Philosophical Essay* (Westminster, 1943), pp. 16ff. and 45ff.

3. Bernard Lonergan, *Insight: A Study of Human Understanding* (London, 1957), p. 678.

4. E. I. Watkin, *The Philosophy of Form* (London, 1935), p. 291.

5. L. Gilkey, *Naming the Whirlwind* (New York: Bobbs- Merrill, 1969), p. 47.

6. George Santayana, *The Realm of Matter* (New York, 1930), pp. 94 and 99.

7. L. Gilkey, *Naming the Whirlwind*, pp. 315–16.

8. Peter Berger, *A Rumor of Angels*, pp. 57–68.

9. Albert Camus, *L'Étranger* (Paris, 1942; ET, S. Gilbert, Middlesex, 1961).

10. Doris Lessing, *Children of Violence*, a five-volume series: *Martha Quest* (New York, 1952); *A Proper Marriage* (New York, 1954); *A Ripple from the Storm* (New York, 1958); *Landlocked* (New York, 1965); and *The Four-Gated City* (New York, 1969). Quotation cited here is taken from *The Four-Gated City*, pp. 61– 62 and 495–96.

11. Romans 7:15-19. Jerusalem Bible translation.

12. Quoted by John Shea, *Stories of God: An Unauthorized Biography* (Chicago, 1978), p. 143.

13. Anna Blaman, quoted in *A New Catechism: The Catholic Faith for Adults* (translation of *De Nieuwe Katechismus*, a book commissioned by the hierarchy of the Netherlands and produced by the Higher Catechetical Institute [Nijmegen, 1965; ET, London, 1959]), pp. 260-61.

14. Daniel Berrigan, *Portraits of Those I Love* (New York, 1982), p. 135.

15. Doris Lessing, *The Golden Notebook* (New York, 1962), pp. 3 and 666.

16. Langdon Gilkey, *Naming the Whirlwind*, pp. 376–77.

17. G. K. Chesterton, *The Everlasting Man* (New York, 1955), pp. 112 and 114 (wording has been slightly changed to make the language inclusive and to put the verbs into the present tense).

18. Eric Mascall, *Existence and Analogy*, p. 85.

Part III

*Recovering the Ancient Instinct
for Astonishment: A Concrete Praxis*

seven

Some Contemporary Spiritual Exercises

The Need for a Concrete Praxis

Mort Walker and Dik Browne are cartoonists. One of their regular cartoons, "Hi and Lois," appears in American newspapers and depicts the ups and downs of an average middle-class family. One of their strips showed the family on a typical Monday morning.

In the first frame, Hi, the father and an accountant by trade, is on his way to work. Driving in his car, he says to himself: "Another dumb day, going to that same dumb office, to work on those same dumb numbers that I must have worked on a thousand times before!" In the second frame, his wife, Lois, is cleaning a floor and saying to herself: "Another dumb day, cleaning this same dumb house that I must have cleaned a thousand times before!" In the next frame, we see the older children on the school bus. One is saying to the other: "Another dumb day, going to the same dumb school, with the same dumb teachers, working at the same dumb stuff we've been working on for a thousand days already!" Finally, in the last frame, we see the youngest, Trixie, a

159

child of about two, standing in her crib, wide awake, fresh for a new day, her arms up in the air, facing the sun, shouting in joy: *"Another day!"* In her young life, this is not just another dumb day. This is virgin time. New things will happen to her this day, and she is ready to be astonished, ready for God to appear. Small wonder Jesus said that children and those with the heart of a child, will inherit the Kingdom of God. In her attitude we see the meaning of purity of heart.

God is born into life after a gestation period.

Conversely, the adults in that cartoon show muddied awareness, consciousness obsessed by narcissism, pragmatism, and unbridled restlessness. Theirs is the typical consciousness of everyday life and it would be them, not Trixie, who would laugh at Nietzsche's madman as he searches for God at high noon in the market square. When we have lost our instinct for astonishment, when we meet the weekday morning with a complaining groan, it should come as no surprise to us that a God whom Jesus says reveals himself to the heart of a child will not be easily perceived. We lack the purity of heart to see God.

I did my doctoral thesis on the classical proofs for the existence of God. Many times, then, I have been asked: "Can you prove that God exists?" "What value do theoretical proofs for God's existence have anyway?" Most people have a healthy skepticism about any attempt rationally to prove that God exists.

Whether or not such skepticism is justified, the instinct behind it says something quite important: God will not be found at the conclusion of a rational syllogism or a mathematical equation. God comes into our world, into our minds and into our hearts as Christ did when he was born in Bethlehem. God is born into life after a gestation period. If someone says to me: "Try to prove to me that God exists!" I would not spend much time trying. Instead I would tell him to live life in a certain way, to approach reality and relationships with a certain set of attitudes. I believe that by doing this they would, like Mary, the mother of Jesus, eventually give birth to God in their lives. The solution to the atheism of our time is not finding better proofs for God's existence but finding a proper way of living, a proper *praxis.* If we live in purity of heart, God will become real. What will help us live in such a way that we prove the existence of God to ourselves?

Purity of heart is the heart seeing, feeling, and relating through the prism of love. Hugo of St. Victor, a twelfth-century theologian, taught that we see correctly by putting love into the heart and mind. He distilled a complete Christian epistemology into one axiom: *Love is the eye.* We see others and the world as they really are when we see them through the eyes of love.

Our task then is to meet life with the bias of the beatitudes, the eye of love. Langdon Gilkey calls this a "preontology."[1] Just as we need healthy lungs to interrelate physically with the world, so too we need healthy symbolic lungs—a proper set of attitudes and habits—to interrelate contemplatively.

Attitudes and Habits

Receptivity and Gratitude

There's a Jewish folk-tale about a young man who aspired to great holiness. After some time working to achieve it, he went to see his Rabbi.

"Rabbi," he announced, "I think I have achieved sanctity."

"Why do you think that?" asked the Rabbi.

———————————— ❧ ————————————

*God has told Adam and Eve that they may
receive life as gift, but they may never take life
as if it were theirs by right.*

"Well," replied the young man, "I've been practicing virtue and discipline for some time and I have grown quite proficient at them. From the time the sun rises until it sets, I take no food or water. All day long, I do all kinds of hard work for others and I never expect to be thanked. If I have temptations of the flesh, I roll in the snow or the thorn bushes until they go away, and then at night, before bed, I practice an ancient monastic discipline and administer lashes to my bare back. I have disciplined myself so as to be holy."

The Rabbi was silent for a time. Then he took the young man by the arm and led him to the window and pointed to an old horse which was just being led away by its master.

"I have been observing that horse for some time," the Rabbi said, "and I have noticed that it doesn't get fed or watered from morning to night. All day long it has to do work for people and it never gets thanked. I often see it rolling around in the snow or bushes, as horses are prone to do, and frequently I see it get whipped. But, I ask you: is that a saint or a horse?"

To be a saint is to be motivated by gratitude, nothing more and nothing less. Gratitude is the root of all virtue. It lies at the base of love and charity. Scripture always and everywhere makes this point.

The original sin of Adam and Eve, the prototype of all sin, is presented as a failure to be receptive and grateful. Scripture scholars tell us that the story of the fall of our first parents, as it appears in Genesis 2–3, was written many years after the Ten Commandments were set down, and that the condition that God gives to Adam and Eve, and which they violate, contains in it all the commandments.

God makes Adam and Eve and places them in the garden and showers them with goodness and life. They are given gift beyond measure and are promised that life will continue in this rich and good way on one condition—they are not to eat the fruit of a certain tree.

The prohibition boils down to this: God has told Adam and Eve that they may *receive* life as gift, but they may never *take* life as if it were theirs by right. The condition God places on them is not an arbitrary or petty test. No. It expresses an entire morality: as long as you receive and respect reality as gift it will continue to give you life and goodness. If you attempt to seize it or take it as owed, you will know shame, disharmony, pain, death, and loss of a connection with God.

Reality, like love, can only be received as gift. Any attempt to take it forcibly, as ours by right, is rape. Adam and Eve's sin was taking by force something that can only be received as gift. This is why the story is laden with sexual metaphor.

Theologian James Mackey tells the true story of a man on a hunting excursion in Africa.[2] He left camp one morning and hiked alone for several miles into the jungle where he surprised and eventually bagged several wild crane. Buckling his catch to his belt, he headed back to camp. At one point, however, he sensed he was being followed. Momentarily frightened, he stopped and looked around. Following him at a distance was a naked and obviously starved adolescent boy. Seeing the boy and his hunger and need, the man stopped, unbuckled his belt, and, letting the cranes fall to the ground, backed off and gestured to the boy that he could take the birds. The boy ran up to the birds but, inexplicably, refused to pick them up. He seemed to be asking for something. Perplexed, the man tried with both words and gestures to explain to the boy that he could take the birds. Still the boy refused to pick them up. Finally, in desperation, unable to explain what he needed, the boy backed away from the dead birds and stood with outstretched arms and open hands . . . waiting until the man came and placed the birds in his hands. He had, despite hunger, fear, and intense need, refused to take the birds; he waited until they were given to him. Only then did he take them. This is the flip side of the story of the fall of Adam and Eve. Just as their story depicts the prototype of all sin, so this one demonstrates the prototype of all virtue. To be a saint is never to take anything as owed, but to receive everything as gift.

Receptivity and gratitude are at the root of purity of heart. They are the real beatitudes. Matthew 5:8 could just as easily be rendered: "Blessed are those who are grateful, who see and appreciate everything as gift, for they shall see God."

But gratitude, like all virtues, is the result of discipline.[3] An earlier generation expressed it this way: *Count your blessings.* To become grateful, one must practice the asceticism of joy. The greatest compliment one can offer the giver of a gift is to thoroughly delight in his gift. We owe it to our creator to delight in the gift of life and creation.

The first exercise we must do to restore our contemplative faculty to its full powers is to work at receiving everything—life, health, the people around us, love, friendship, food, drink, sexuality, beauty—as gift. Becoming a more grateful person is the first and the most important step in overcoming the practical atheism that besets our everyday lives. To the extent that we take life for granted we will never see the Giver behind the gift. But once we stop taking life for granted we will begin to feel it as a gift from God.

A Sense of Divine Providence

In *The Last Temptation of Christ,* Nikos Kazantzakis puts the following homily into Christ's mouth:

> Jesus's eyes flashed. Though he was in front of such a great multitude, his heart felt no fear. He parted his lips. "Brothers," he shouted, "open your ears, open your hearts—I ran here . . . to announce the happy news for the first time.

What happy news? The Kingdom of God has come!"

An old man with a double hump like a camel's lifted his chaplet and cackled, "Vague words, the words you speak, son of the carpenter, vague, groundless words. 'Kingdom of heaven,' 'justice,' 'freedom,' and 'grab what you can boys, it's all for the taking.' I've had enough! Miracles, miracles! I want you to do something here and now. Perform some miracles to make us believe in you. Otherwise, shut up!"

"Everything is a miracle, old man," Jesus replied. "What further miracles do you want? Look below you: even the humblest blade of grass has its guardian angel who stands by and helps it to grow. Look above you: what a miracle is the star-filled sky! And if you close your eyes, old man, what a miracle the world within us! What a star-filled sky is our heart!"

The people listened to him, and the clay within them turned into wings. The entire time this betrothal lasted, if you lifted a stone you found God underneath, if you knocked on a door, God came out to open it for you, if you looked in the eye of your friend or your enemy, you saw God sitting in the pupil and smiling at you.[4]

Karl Rahner was once asked whether he believed in miracles. He replied, "I don't believe in miracles, I *rely* on them to get me through each day." We, too, need to have a vital sense of divine providence in our lives. When we have that, as Kazantzakis's story goes, every time we lift a stone we will find God underneath it.

In the tradition of philosophical theism this is achieved by having a proper sense of contingency in our lives. Jesus had his own expression for it. He called it "reading the signs of the times." How do we do that?

Some years ago, a woman in a class I was teaching shared this story. She had been raised in a religious home and had been a pious and regular churchgoer. During her years at university, however, her interest in and practice of religion had progressively slipped. By the time she graduated she no longer attended church or prayed. This indifference continued for several years after her graduation.

One day, some four years later, she flew to Colorado to visit her married sister and to ski. She arrived on a Saturday evening. The next morning, her sister invited her to go to Mass with her. She politely refused and went skiing instead. On her first run down the ski-slope she hit a tree and broke her leg. Sporting a huge cast, she was released from the hospital the following Saturday. The next morning, her sister again invited her to come to Mass with her. This time, since "there wasn't anything else to do," she accepted the invitation.

As luck would have it, it was Good Shepherd Sunday. As chance would have it, there happened to be a priest visiting from Israel. He could not see her sitting in the pews, yet he began his homily this way:

"There is a custom among shepherds in Israel that existed at the time of Jesus and is still practiced today that needs to be understood in order to appreciate this text. Sometimes very early on in the life of a lamb, a shepherd senses that it is going to be a congenital stray, one forever drifting away from the herd. What the shepherd does is take the lamb and deliberately break its leg so that he has to carry it until its leg is healed. By that time, the lamb has become so attached to the shepherd that it never strays again."

"I may be dense!" concluded this woman, "but given my broken leg and this coincidence, hearing this woke up something inside me. Fifteen years have passed since then, and I have prayed and gone to church regularly ever since!"

John of the Cross once said that the language of God is the experience that God writes into our lives.[5] James Mackey, quoting George Santayana, suggests that divine providence is *a conspiracy of accidents.* What this woman experienced that Sunday was the language of God, divine providence, acting through a conspiracy of accidents. In her response, she read the signs of the times.

Today, the concept of divine providence is not very popular. Our age tends to see it as an unhealthy fatalism ("If God wants my child to live he won't let him die! We won't take the blood transfusion!"), an unhealthy fundamentalism ("God sent AIDS into the world as a punishment for our sexual promiscuity!"), or an unhealthy theology of God ("God sends us natural and personal disasters to bring us back to true values!"). For the most part, it is good that our age rejects such false concepts of providence. God does not start fires, or floods, or wars, or AIDs, or anything else of this nature in order to wake us up. Nature, chance, human freedom, and human sin bring these things to pass.

However, to say that God does not initiate or cause these things is not the same thing as saying that God does not speak through them. God is in these chance events, both in the disastrous ones and in the advantageous ones, and speaks through them. Past generations more easily understood this.

For example, my parents were farmers. For them, as for Abraham and Sarah of old, there were no accidents—there was only providence. If they had good crops, God was blessing them. If they had poor crops, well, they concluded that God, for reasons they should try to grasp and understand, wanted them to live on less for a while. For them, there was no ordinary secular reality. Divine providence was always seen in the conspiracy of accidents that constituted ordinary life. They always tried to read the signs of the times. They stood before every event, good or bad, personal or communal, and asked the question: "What is God saying to us?"

ᘜ

God is in these chance events, both in
the disastrous ones and in the advantageous
ones, and speaks through them.

In prayer and discernment, they would always figure out those reasons in the depths of their hearts. This is what mysticism looks like in ordinary life, the mysticism Rahner points to when he says he relies on miracles to get him through each day. To have a sense of God's presence in everyday life, we don't need the kind of miracles that drastically change ordinary reality and prove beyond the shadow of a doubt that there is a supernatural world beyond our natural world (a miracle in the common sense understanding). No. We need a deeper sense that God is already present and acting in the seemingly ordinary events of our lives. We need to read the signs of the times. When we find a penny on the street, we need to feel that God is blessing us. Then we are mystics.

Learning to see the finger of God, divine providence, in the big and small events of our daily lives is the second major spiritual exercise we must do to move beyond our practical atheism.

Self-Abandonment and Obedience unto Death

There is a contemporary parable about a Cretan peasant, a man who deeply loved his life and work. He enjoyed tilling the soil, feeling the warm sun on his naked back as he worked in the fields, and feeling the dirt under his feet. He loved the planting, the harvesting, the very smell of nature. He loved especially his wife, his children and his friends, and he enjoyed being with them, eating together, drinking wine, talking, making love, and simply being united in a shared life. And he loved Crete, his tiny country. The earth, the sky, the sea, it was his!

One day he sensed that death was near. We was not afraid of the beyond, for he had lived a good life. No. But he feared leaving Crete, his wife, his children, his friends, his home, and his land. As he prepared to die, he grasped a few grams of soil from his beloved Crete in his hand and told his loved ones to bury him with it.

He died, awoke, and found himself at heaven's gate, the soil still in his hand and heaven's gate firmly barred against him. Eventually St. Peter came through the heavy gates and addressed him: "You've lived a good life, and we have a place for you inside, but you cannot enter unless you drop that handful of soil." "Why? Why must I let go of this soil? I will not! What's inside those gates I don't know. But this soil I know—it's my life, my wife, my work, my family, it's all that I know and love, it's Crete! I will not let it go!"

A silent Peter left him and closed the large gates behind him. There seemed little point in arguing with the peasant. Several minutes later, the gates opened a second time and this time a very young child emerged. She did not try to reason with the man, nor did she try to coax him into letting go of the soil in his hand. She simply took his hand and, as she did, the soil of Crete spilled to the ground. Then she led him through the gates of heaven. A shock awaited the man as he entered heaven. There before him lay all of Crete.[6]

This parable illustrates what Jesus meant when he said that love demands "obedience unto death." It demands that we let go of what we cling to instinctually so as to be able to receive that very thing in its reality and fullness. To be obedient to love, to give oneself over to it, means always hearing the call to self-sacrifice, to self-abandonment.

The contemplative traditions we outlined previously all make this point. The mystics tell us that we come to purity of heart by moving beyond ourselves; the Protestant tradition that it lies in submission to the Holy; and the tradition of philosophical theism that we are always acting under obedience to some God. Purity of heart will only come when we give ourselves over to something above us.

Jesus expresses this in his own way at the end of John's gospel. After asking Peter three times: "Do you love me?" and being assured by Peter that he does, Jesus says to him: "When you were younger, you girded your belt and walked wherever you wished; but when you grow old, you will stretch out your hands, and someone else will gird you, and bring you to where you would rather not go."[7] Part of the essence of love, of any life of true self-giving, is obedience—being led by something and Somebody outside oneself to where one would rather not go. Dag Hammarskjold, in a famous entry in his diaries, put it this way: "I don't know who—or what— put the question, I don't know when it was put. I don't even remember answering. But at some moment I did answer yes to someone—or something—and from that hour I was certain that existence is meaningful and that, therefore, my life, in self-surrender, had a goal."[8]

The road beyond the practical atheism of our everyday consciousness lies in self-abandonment. If John of the Cross were your spiritual director and you went to him with the complaint that God did not seem very alive or real to you, he would prescribe this exercise: "As unpopular as this advice might be in a world that tells you to do your own thing, bend your will according to the beatitudes of Jesus. Stand before your loved ones and before your God and practice saying what Jesus said to his Father in the garden: 'Not my will, but yours, be done.' Then come back in a few years and tell me whether God still seems absent from your life."

Second Naivete

If you ask a naive child, "Do you believe in Santa Claus?" he will say yes. If you ask a bright child the same question, he will say no. If you ask an even brighter child that question, he will reply yes, though for a different reason.

This little vignette is a prescriptive counsel for the restoration of wonder within our lives. A contemplative consciousness, one that is truly attuned to the full depth and mystery within reality, not only wonders how but it especially wonders at, with the eyes, the mind, and the heart of a child and a virgin.

To perceive what is most primitive and primordial in reality, we need a primitive spirit; to perceive virginal truth, we need a virginal spirit; and to see the truth about the childhood of the world, we need to see the world with childlike directness. To come to purity of heart we must strive to live in a second naivete[9] and to revirginize daily.

Revirginization is the process of continually recapturing the posture of a child before reality; second naivete describes that posture as it exists in an adult who has moved beyond the natural naivete of a child but is not lost in the deserts of cynicism, criticism, and false sophistication. It is post-critical, post-adult, post-sophisticated.

As children we are natural contemplatives. We spontaneously wonder at things and see things with directness. Reality is naturally mysterious, and all too full of the aesthetic and the supernatural. Prior to the critical judgments that come with sophistication, little children perceive the world as laden with beauty and spirits. It is easy for them to believe in angels, ghosts, and other supernatural and mythical things. Only as we mature, grow more critical, and approach reality with more *a priori* filters do we grow skeptical and begin to despoil the world of its aesthetic, mysterious, romantic, and supernatural dimensions.

This is a necessary process. A child's natural contemplative faculties are based upon a naivete that would hardly be an ideal quality in an adult. As we grow to maturity, it is for our own good that our critical and practical faculties sharpen. But this growth is itself not an end, but part of a process of further development. Beyond the loss of natural naivete and contemplativeness lies another kind of awareness, second naivete, which sees again with the directness of a child, but has now integrated into that posture the critical and practical concerns of an adult. In natural naivete we are childish; in second naivete we are childlike.

Unfortunately in our post-modern and very sophisticated culture, the critical faculty that destroys our initial naivete is taken as an end in itself. We are life-smart and proud of it. Like Adam and Eve after the fall, our eyes are opened. We have a proclivity for cynicism since life holds few surprises, taboos, or sacred dimensions. Atheism and idolatry have their basis there.

If we want a more real sense of God in our lives we must move towards second naivete. We must touch the nerve of novelty, purging ourselves of Chesterton's illusion of familiarity, and learn to see things as if we were seeing them for the first time. The answer to atheism and agnosticism is not a closed mind, but an open one. We move towards this higher agnosticism when we deliberately and consciously attempt to purge ourselves of cynicism, contempt, and every attitude, however subtle and unconscious, that identifies mystery with ignorance.

This notion can best be captured by poetry. Again, let me quote G. K. Chesterton:

When all my days are ending
And I have no song to sing,
I think that I shall not be too old
To stare at everything;
As I stared once at a nursery door
Or a tall tree and a swing . . .

Men grow too old for love, my love,
Men grow too old for lies;
But I shall not grow too old to see
Enormous night arise,
A cloud that is larger than the world
And a monster made of eyes . . .
Men grow too old to woo, my love,
Men grow too old to wed:
But I shall not grow too old to see
Hung crazily overhead
Incredible rafters when I wake
And I find that I am not dead . . .

Strange crawling carpets of the grass,
Wide window of the sky:
So in this perilous grace of God
With all my sins go I:
And things grow new though I grow old,
Though I grow old and die.[10]

What type of *praxis* leads us toward a second naivete?
Two metaphors are particularly helpful.

Imagine a terrain that has been ravaged by natural
disaster and despoiled by human beings. Its waters are

polluted, its vegetation is dead, and its natural beauty is destroyed. However, given time and weather—sun, rain, winds, storms, frost and snow—it will revirginize. Its waters will grow clear and pure, vegetation will sprout, and its natural beauty will return. It becomes new again. So, too, our hearts, our minds, our souls, and our bodies: when we stop despoiling them with the attitude that thinks it already understands everything, they will gradually regain their virginity and begin to blush again at the very wonder of knowing and loving. A chastity in perception will return.

Now imagine the gestation process in the womb. The process begins with a microscopic egg, a cellular speck,

*Atheism questions too little, and
it examines too narrowly.*

which is being formed, cared for, and shaped by the things around it, nourished by a reality that is infinitely larger than itself. The process takes place in darkness. Eventually the child grows sufficiently and emerges from the darkness, opens her eyes to the light, and sees this world for the first time. The sheer overwhelmingness of what it sees so overpowers the child that it takes years of time for the child's senses and mind to begin to understand. But initially the child just looks and wonders. So too the process of being reborn to second naivete, to new virginity. We must, metaphorically speaking, make a recessive journey, a voyage to the sources, to the fetal darkness of the womb, and be gestated anew so that we can again open our eyes and see a reality that is so wild, so startling, and so overpowering that we are reduced to silence, able only to wonder.

Second naivete is not a posture that wilfully blinds itself to hard reality and refuses to ask the tough questions. It is genuinely agnostic, fully open to wonder, and knows so little of a rich and multifarious reality that there just might be a Santa Claus after all.

And there might be a God after all! Atheism is not, as we so popularly imagine, the result of the human race coming of age and having the courage to rid ourselves of fairy tales and superstitions. Atheism, for the most part, is rooted in the opposite. It questions too little, and it examines too narrowly. Jesus tells us that it is children who will see God.

To exercise our contemplative muscles, we must work at regaining the wonder, awe, and openness of a child. If Jesus was my spiritual director and I came to him complaining that the sense of God was habitually absent within my everyday experience, he would challenge me to get into more vital contact with the little boy and the virgin inside me.

The Practice of Contemplation

There is a parable about our search for God. There was a little fish who swam up to his mother one day and asked: "Mummy, where is this water that I hear so much about?"

The mother replied: "You stupid little fish! It's all about you and in you. Just swim up on the beach and lie there for a while and you'll find out."

And so the person who is searching for God. One day she walks up to her spiritual director and says: "Where is this God that I hear so much about?"[11]

The parable ends there. God is to us like the ocean is to fish, all around us and in us. In God we live and move and have our being. If we can never get outside God how can we keep ourselves aware of God's reality? If we are swimming in God but he does not seem as real to us as the heartaches and headaches of our daily lives, how can we make ourselves more aware of him?

Classical spiritual authors, not just in Christianity but in all the major world religions, suggest that one of the ways out of this dilemma is the practice of contemplative prayer. This, to cite just one example, is the basis of the famous fourteenth-century English mystical treatise *The Cloud of Unknowing.* It is also a strong motif in many of the writings emerging today from the post-Merton Trappist communities.[12] The Cistercians generally call this "Centering Prayer," but what they advocate is in fact what older classical authors call contemplation.

In classical Christian spirituality, there are two essential ways of praying: meditation and contemplation. Very early on in Christian spiritual writings, as we've seen, authors distinguished between *praxis* and *theoria. Praxis* refers to what we can do in our attempt to reach God and others, namely, works of charity and justice, discursive prayer, and ascetical practices. *Theoria* refers to what happens within us when God and others were actually encountered. Hence, *praxis* refers to what is active and *theoria* to what is receptive and passive.

Prayer is called meditation when we are active within it. You decide to spend a half hour in prayer. You sit down in a quiet place and pick up the Bible. You find a text you want to meditate on and begin your prayer. You read the text slowly and try to let it speak to you. It does. You begin to feel consolation from God, challenge from God, sorrow for your sins, joy in being blessed by God. You feel yourself becoming more insightful. You pray for others. But you also experience distractions. Every so often, your mind wanders and you catch yourself thinking about other things—your heartaches and headaches. When these distractions occur, you catch yourself and bring yourself back to what you are praying about. All this activity, all this *praxis,* is meditation.

Contemplation, or centering prayer, is quite different. Unlike meditation, which is an exercise in concentration, contemplation is an exercise in refusing to concentrate on anything, including holy thoughts and divine inspirations. You decide to spend a half hour in prayer. You sit down in a quiet place. You do not bring the Bible, nor do you bring anything to pray on or about. You begin contemplating by making a brief act of meditation. You actively focus yourself on what you are about to do, pray, and tell God that you are here to pray, that this next half hour will be prayer. Then you calm and center yourself, perhaps using a breathing technique and a prayer word (though these are optional). Then you begin to contemplate. What do you do? Nothing. You let your heart and mind go and you interfere in the stream of feelings and consciousness only when you catch yourself concentrating very long on anything, including holy thoughts and divine inspirations. In contemplation there is no distinction between distractions and holy thoughts. You try to hang onto God by refusing to hang onto anything else, including thoughts and feelings about God. The whole time of prayer, save for a very brief explicit act of meditation at the beginning and again at the end, consists of this stream of consciousness and feeling.

But how is this prayer? And how will it make us more aware of God? Let us return to the parable of the fish and the ocean.

Imagine you are the mother fish and your child comes to you and says: "Mummy, where is this water we hear so much about?" To give your child some sense of water, even though it is totally immersed within it, you could set up a slide projector at the bottom of the ocean and show your child pictures of water. (Since this is a parable and anything is possible, you could do this.) As ironic as it would be, these pictures, which are not water, would in fact give your child, who is living in water, some idea of what water is. Eventually, after having shown your child hours of pictures of water, you turn off all the TVs and the slide projector and tell the child: "Now that you have some idea of what water is, I want you to sit in it and let it flow through you." Our new parable demonstrates the difference between mediation and contemplation of God.

All thoughts and feelings about God, even scripture itself, are not God. Good as they are, they are not the reality. At a point, they must give way to the reality. Meditation must give way to contemplation. Instead of thinking and feeling *about* God we must sit *in* God. Meditation is watching the slides. It brings concepts, thoughts, and feelings about the reality. Contemplation is sitting in the reality. Normally it does not feel like prayer.

Suppose you are sitting in contemplative prayer regularly. How do you know whether you are actually praying or wasting your time? Unlike meditation, you do not make any assessment during or after prayer. You do contemplative prayer for a substantial period of time, several months perhaps, and then check yourself: Am I now more restful than restless? More free than compulsive? More calm than hyper? More patient than impatient? More humble than competitive? More self-forgetful than self-preoccupied? More grateful than bitter? If there is progress in these things, then I am praying and God is more vitally in my life.

If a sense of God's presence is absent within our lives, more than likely restlessness, obsessions, impatience, competitiveness, self-preoccupation, and bitterness are not absent. Small wonder God cannot break in! Contemplative prayer, practiced regularly as a discipline, is an invaluable exercise for purifying awareness.

Kissing the Leper

A story about Francis of Assisi, perhaps more mythical than factual, illustrates how touching the poor is the cure for a mediocre or dying faith:

One night prior to his conversion, Francis, then a rich and pampered young man, donned his flashiest clothes, mounted his horse, and set off for a night of drinking and carousing. God, social justice, and the poor were not on his mind. Riding down a narrow road, he found his path blocked by a leper. Francis was particularly repulsed by the deformities and smell of lepers. He tried to steer his horse around the him, but the path was too narrow. Frustrated, angry, but with his path clearly blocked, Francis had no other choice but to get down off his horse and try to move the leper out of his path. When he put out his hand and touched the leper's arm, something inside him snapped. Undeterred by the smell of rotting flesh and unashamed, he kissed that leper and his life was never the same again. In that kiss, Francis found the reality of God and of love in a way that changed him forever.

Many of us struggle with the same issues as the pre-converted Francis, with a pampered life and a mediocre and dying faith. We know that our faith calls us to work for social justice and that this demand is non-negotiable. We know, too, as somebody once put it with a praiseworthy succinctness, that strength without compassion is violence; that compassion without justice is weakness; that justice without love is Marxism; and that love without justice is baloney! What we don't know is that the preferential option for the poor is the cure for our mediocre and dying faith. We must kiss the leper.

If we touch the poor we touch Christ. Touching the poor can be a functional substitute for prayer and, given the culture we live in, we need this substitute.

Western culture today is so powerful and alluring that it often swallows us whole. Its beauty, power, and promise generally take away both our breath and our perspective. The lure of present salvation—money, sex, creativity, the good life—has, for the most part, entertained, amused, distracted, and numbed us into a state where we no longer have a perspective beyond that of our culture and its short-range soteriology.

One way out of this, of course, is through prayer. A life of prayer can cure a dying faith. The problem is that our life of prayer is precisely what our culture erodes in us. It is the hardest thing to sustain in our lives today.

Everything militates against it. Perhaps the only way we have of not letting ourselves be swallowed whole by our culture is to kiss the leper, to place our lot with those who have no within it, namely, the poor with their many faces: the aged, the sick, the dying, the unborn, the handicapped, the unattractive, the displaced. To touch those who have no place in our culture is to give ourselves a perspective beyond our culture.

Daniel Berrigan describes in his memoirs how much his perspective changed when he began to work full-time in a cancer ward ministering to the terminally ill. When you walk home from work after a day with people who are dying, he says, your vision clears pretty well and what your culture offers no longer seems so irresistible. Concrete contact with the poor is Christian contemplation. It knocks the scales off one's eyes.

"Whatsoever you do to the least of my people, that you do unto me," Christ assures us. God is ever-present in our world in the face of the poor, waiting to be met. In the powerless, one can find the power of God; in the voiceless, one can hear the voice of God; in the impoverished, one can find God's treasures; in the weak, one can find God's strength; and in the unattractive, one can find God's beauty. The glory of God might indeed be humanity fully alive, but the privileged presence of God lies with the poor who are not fully alive in the eyes of our culture.

Like Francis, we need to get off our horses and kiss the leper. If we do, something will snap, we will see our pampered lives for what they are, and God and love will break into our lives in such a way that we will never be the same again.

The Contuition of God
in Everyday Life

A hundred years ago, Nietzsche's mythical madman smashed a lantern in the marketplace at high noon and announce to Western culture that "God is dead!" Few people took Nietzsche very seriously because, at that time, God was still very much alive in the Christian churches even if he was quite dead in everyday life. Today, the children of Western culture, we struggle with practical atheism. Our churches are slowly emptying and more and more the sense of God slips from our ordinary lives.

This problem with God stems not from the fact that we are any less sincere or moral than previous generations, but from the fact that, for reasons whose roots go back hundreds of years, our consciousness is so clouded with self-centeredness, practicality, and restlessness that we are contemplatively asleep. We need to do contemplative exercises if we are to regain a vital sense of God.

The road back, however, is not through a better rational and intellectual apologetic for the existence of God. Nobody is ever going to prove to anyone that God exists and that the only rational option is faith. To quote Shakespeare somewhat out of context, proofs for the existence of God only "help to thicken other proofs that do demonstrate thinly."[13] Nor is the road back through miracles, apparitions, healings, Marian appearances, or extraordinary religious experiences. The God of ordinary life will be found in the ordinary.

The road back to a lively faith is not about answers, but about living in a certain way—contemplatively.

Blessed are those who do not take life for granted, for they are within measurable distance of taking it as granted to them by God.

Blessed are those who learn to see the finger of God in the conspiracy of accidents that make up their lives; they shall be rewarded with daily miracles.

Blessed are those who say yes to something higher than themselves; in that genuflection they will say the creed.

Blessed are those who take on the heart of a child and the heart of a virgin; they shall again delight in Santa Claus and believe in God.

===================== ⟨⟨ =====================

The God of ordinary life
will be found in the ordinary.

Blessed are those whose discipleship includes the discipline of regular prayer; they shall know that it is in God that they live and move and have their being.

Blessed are those who kiss a leper, who make the preferential option for the poor, for love and God will overwhelm them.

And blessed are those who make this a life-long quest; they will make a good beginning.

Notes

1. Langdon Gilkey, *Reaping the Whirlwind*, pp. 103–4.

2. This is Mackey's central idea in the Eucharistic theology he gives in "Anticipatory Incompletions," in *The Christian Experience of*

God as Trinity (London: SCM Press, 1983), pp. 255–58. The story itself, however, while illustrating his central idea, is not given in the book cited. It was given as an illustration as part of his lectures on the theology of the Trinity, University of San Francisco, Summer 1979.

3. Henri Nouwen, in his work *Life of the Beloved* (New York: Crossroad, 1992) lays out simply and clearly the disciplines required to become and remain grateful. See especially pp. 55–68.

4. Nikos Kazantzakis, *The Last Temptation of Christ* (New York: Simon and Schuster, 1960), pp. 189 and 301.

5. John of the Cross, *The Living Flame of Love,* commentary on stanza one, number 7. My expression is a paraphrase. His actual wording is: "For God's speech is the effect he produces in the soul" (Kavanaugh, *op. cit.,* p. 582).

6. I heard this story, in roughly this form, from John Shea. I am uncertain of his source, though it seems to be a redaction and re-mythologization of what Nikos Kazantzakis says about his own life in his autobiography, *Report to Greco* (New York: Simon and Schuster, 1960).

7. John 21:18.

8. Dag Hammarskjold, *Markings,* translated by Leif Sjorberg and W. H. Auden (London: Faber and Faber, 1964), p. 85.

9. I have taken the term *second naivete* from Paul Ricoeur, though my usage of the term is not, always and everywhere, the same as his.

10. G. K. Chesterton, "A Second Childhood," quoted by Eric Mascall, *Words and Images: A Study in Theological Discourse* (London, 1957), p. 81.

11. Thomas Keating, *Finding Grace at the Center* (Still River, Mass., 1978), pp. 34–35.

12. I recommend especially two books by Thomas Keating, *Finding Grace at the Center* (note 17, above) and *Open Mind, Open Heart: The Contemplative Dimension of the Gospel* (Amity, N.Y.: Amity House, 1986). Both lay out a good practical method of doing centering prayer.

13. William Shakespeare, *Othello,* III. iii.

Reflection Guide
The Shattered Lantern

This guide, prepared by The Crossroad Publishing Company, is for use by individuals for private reflection, and for small reading groups.

Chapter 1

Reflect on the place of God in your own life — your friends, colleagues, church members. What difference does God make for the lives of these people? For your own life?

Chapter 2

a. Reread Rolheiser's description of the walk in the beautiful forest (p. 35). Think of a similar example from your own life, or the life of someone you know, where being preoccupied led someone to overlook what was miraculous and beautiful in their immediate surroundings. What parallel can you find between this kind of overlooking and the way many of us overlook God in our daily lives?

b. "One of the major reasons why we are not more contemplative, why we do not pray more, and why we do not take time to smell the flowers, is that these activities do not accomplish anything" (p. 40). Think about the phrase "contemplative life." Write down several ideas and words you associate with it. What relation to you see between the contemplative life and the life of achievement, hard work, and getting things done? Do they seem opposed, in competition, complementary?

c. Think of one example of how a lack of chastity can make someone restless and distracted. Relate that example to these words (p. 50): "When there is never time or space to stand behind our own lives and look reflectively at them, then the pressures and distractions of life simply consume us to the point where we lose control over our lives."

Chapter 3

a. "If there is a God, we already know all about him" (p. 56). Write down several things you believe about God. (For example, God knows all things; God is just an illusion we create; God is good.) Do your beliefs about God include the possibility that God is beyond our ability to conceive God? Why or why not?

b. "Contemplation is natural to the human person. It is not something we must learn, but something we must relearn, and relearn again, throughout our lives" (p. 65). Take a few minutes to recall the sense of wonder you felt as a child. How does life and the world seem different to you today? How might your vision of

the world, your "eyesight", be different if you redis-
covered that sense of wonder?

Chapter 4

a. Consider the idea that mysticism is an experience
available to everyone. For a moment, try to imagine
yourself as a mystic. What ideas, challenges, and
objections occur to you when you imagine this? What
assumptions do you have about the sort of person
who can be a mystic?

b. Review and restate in your own words the "three
veils" John of the Cross outlines. Consider as well the
three ways of moving beyond the veils. How are they
related?

Chapter 5

a. Reflect on the idea that there is a God who intimately
knows every detail of every event in the universe
(p. 104). Do you find it easy to think that this idea is
true? Do you find it easy to grasp this idea in your
imagination?

b. "Grade-school arithmetic does not disappear when
Einstein appears, a photograph of someone does not
become unreal when you actually see the person, and
a candle still gives off light even when a bright sun
eclipses that light; they remain as the foundation
through which we move on to trust in that which is
greater than they are" (p. 114). Reflect on a time
when your wisdom and intuitive understanding of a

person or situation grew deeper. From the perspective of that deeper wisdom, how did you see the partial wisdom you had already possessed earlier? How does it relate to the fuller wisdom to gained? Do any analogies come to mind to explain this relation? (Examples: part and whole; root and tree.)

Chapter 6

a. Reflect on Rolheiser's discussion of contingency (p. 135). According to the author, does contemplation seem more like a denial of a secular worldview or a development out of it?

b. "All of us, whether we admit it or not, serve some lord, some real or surrogate God" (p. 153). List several events, objects, or people that you or others you know have made into idols. In what ways have you sacrificed to them and worshiped them?

Chapter 7

a. Practice gratitude right now. Think of several people, events, and other things for which you are genuinely grateful, and thank God for them now.

b. "In natural naivete we are childish; in second naivete we are childlike" (p. 174). Now that you've read *The Shattered Lantern,* write down five ways you can apply the practical ideas of this book for your own life. In what ways can you become "childlike"?

About the Author

Hundreds of thousands of readers have been introduced to Ronald Rolheiser through his recent book *The Holy Longing* (Doubleday), a runaway bestseller in Catholic and Protestant circles. His reputation had already been growing steadily for decades, on the strength of a series of books around the issues of spirituality, theology, and modernity, all concerned with reawakening the fire of spirituality for people who sense its absence, or are not even aware of it. These earlier books include *Against an Infinite Horizon: The Finger of God in Our Everyday Lives* and *The Shattered Lantern: Rediscovering a Felt Presence of God*, presented here.

Fr. Rolheiser, a Roman Catholic priest, is the General Councillor for Canada for his order, the Oblates of Mary Immaculate. He as a community-builder, teacher, and writer, with offices in Toronto and Rome. He received his STD from the University of Louvain, Belgium; for most of the twenty-eight years of his priesthood, he taught theology and philosophy at Newman Theological College in Edmonton, Alberta. Today he is an adjunct faculty member at Seattle University. Fr. Rolheiser's columns appear in more than fifty newspapers throughout the English-speaking world.

Information about Fr. Rolheiser, including speaking events, books, and recent columns, can be found at www.ronrolheiser.com.